Works

AND OTHER "SMOKY GEORGE" STORIES

BY
PERRY BRASS

Belhue Press

Belhue Press First Edition
Copyright ©1992 by Perry Brass

Published in the United States of America by:

Belhue Press
P.O. Box 1081
Ridgefield, CT 06877-0842

Cover photo, by Jay McLeod, courtesy the Wessel/O'Connor Gallery, NYC. Cover and overall design by M. Fitzhugh.

ISBN 0-9627123-2-9
LIBRARY OF CONGRESS CATALOGUE CARD NUMBER: 92-071426

For Lou Thomas, who took these stories seriously. And for all the other editors I've worked for who cared about Smoky George.

Also, for Hugh, Jeff, Harvis, George and John, and always, for my dear friend, T.R. Witomski.

I would also like to the thank the editors and publishers of *FirstHand Magazine*, who've graciously allowed me to reprint these stories, many of which first appeared in *FirstHand* and *Manscape* in a slightly different form. All of these stories, with the exceptions of "Sex & Violence" (from 1975) and "The Man With the California Face" (1990) have appeared in magazines such as *Torso*, *Honcho*, *Mandate*, *AdvocateMen*, and of course, *FirstHand* and *Manscape*. With the exception of "Sex & Violence," the stories date from 1983 to 1990.

Other books by Perry Brass:

Sex-charge (poetry)

Mirage, a science fiction novel

CONTENTS

... We

are two lonely cowboys—

the suburban imagination

has been

buggered

worse by our leaving together.

from poem "Penis to Nipple,"
Perry Brass 1991

Introduction

What happens when a poet writes "porn?"

He changes things. He spoofs on it, grows in it, and finds a place for his own voice.

For many years, I could not be published in the tony, gay literary magazines that sprang up in the late '70s and into the '80s. I wasn't writing stories about sensitive young men who had trouble with their mothers, or about their coming out. I had written those stories almost 20 years earlier. So I began writing the sex-driven stories gay men love to call "porn." For one thing, they actually paid, and for the second, the editors of "porn" magazines took me more seriously and more professionally than the editors of literary magazines.

I took on the pseudonym "Smoky George," because there was something sort of wild and woolly about the name, and it seemed appropriately distant from me. "Smoky" became a mask that I could talk through, the way that Somerset Maugham invented the spy Ashenden to tell his own espionage stories. Although Maugham did some spying during World War I, he was certainly not as smooth and unrufflable as Ashenden. "Smoky" also seemed to have a life of his own; so much so that the late Lou Thomas, editor of *FirstHand Magazine,* who was a great fan of these stories, wrote to me in 1988, after the stories hadn't appeared for a while: "How nice it is to have Smoky back after a long vacation. I'm going to put him in my briefcase when I go away this weekend, and take him out when I'm in bed tonight. That seems like the right place for him."

Early on, I decided that if I was going to write porn, I was going to write the stories that I wanted—stories about "real men" and their jobs, men who had a hard time paying the rent, who were embarrassed by their own sexual feelings, who were often afraid on the street, but who did not let that keep them from cruising them. Luckily, many of my editors went for them. They liked the idea that the men in my stories were more "real," weren't all twenty-two and built like studs, and had real thoughts and problems. They also liked the idea that "Smoky," the narrator of the stories, became a character in his own right. He was older, had been around the block many times, and had a definite voice. Sometimes, they objected to the issues that I brought up, like race, physical handicap, and class differences. But often they were intrigued by putting these issues in stories in magazines that got little credit from the "literati," but which were the real gay connection for many, many men.

In many ways, these stories are documentations of a different time. Before AIDS (you may notice a terrible amount of unsafe sex in them; the stories were never meant as sex manuals, but fantasy fulfillments), a time when gay men cruised more and networked less, and when we could be more openly—amazingly—kind to strangers. What I wanted to keep out of my stories was contempt for tender, vulnerable feelings as well as sex negativeness. What I wanted to put in was a voice many men could hear and understand: sexually uninhibited, but conscious of life's problems and dilemmas. I also wanted them to be funny, and this was often difficult: porn is supposed to make you hot, not laugh. But I think fun is as important a part of sex as mystery is, and I wanted some of both.

Now that I read these stories again, they open up a very different time for me, and many of the men who figured so much in them—as editors, friends, and supporters—are no longer with us. But gay writing is getting the kind of support it merits, and that writing should include sexually explicit writing as well the kind of stuff that now can charm its way into *The New Yorker*. I do see that the variety of experiences we have are limitless, and that there are as many gay stories to tell as there are Jewish stories or black stories or stories of any group.

Almost fifteen years ago, I suggested to a prominent New York gay editor that gay literature should be considered another genre of literature, like Jewish literature. He said to me, "Yes, but how long have the Jews had literature?" It did not occur to him that the Bible was literature, and that literature was not invented with the novel. It is this sort of thinking which limits gay writing a great deal, and I'm glad to say that I haven't been part of those limits, and neither has Smoky George.

W ORKS

I'd been eyeing Works, the foreman on the ranch outside of Modesto, all week. I'd been eyeing him and there were certain times he'd look at me and my knees went watery. He was tall and built like a cedar telephone pole— all muscle and fiber. Not bony, but beautiful, long muscles. It was the second evening we'd found ourselves stripped naked together. We were washing off in the irrigation canal a good way from the bunkhouse, after dusty work in the apricot fields we were refencing. It was a nice time for me to be doing that kind of work, some years ago when I thought I had time in my life to burn. I must have put on five pounds of muscle in that first week. And I'll tell you—with the heat of working in the fields and the hard work itself, I was itchy and horny to get at Works.

He suddenly swam over to me in the dark, cool water. You couldn't drink it, but it was clean enough to wash in. Secretly, I knew I had a hard-on. I felt embarrassed and excited at the same time. The tip of my dick was starting to quiver, and there was a certain point where I knew I just couldn't hold back or hide it anymore. I got down further in the water.

"This sure feels good," Works said to me, and he grabbed the large bar of Ivory Soap drifting beside him. They were right, it did "float." He stood up. His cock, fairly long and skinny, but with a great, kind of baseball of a head, hung limply down him. He soaped himself quickly, but then spent a lot of time at his nuts.

"That looks like fun," I said.

"Yeh. I like playing with them," he grinned sheepishly.

I thought I was going to pass out in the water. I could see the newspaper headlines the next day: "Man Drowns from Horniness."

I decided then I was too far gone to hold back. He could fire me, throw me off the ranch, and I'd have to head back, defeated, to San Francisco. If things got really rough and he started to give me a hard time—well, I knew if I had to, I could try to beat the shit out of him. Or die trying. But at least I'd get one chance to put my hands on him. Then he could make up his mind as to what *he* really wanted.

I grabbed the Ivory when he let go of it in the water. When he turned away from me, I started to soap down his back.

"Like this?" I asked. He didn't answer, and I felt myself sigh from the pleasure of feeling his muscles under the pressure of my hands. His back was tight and ripply. It started to loosen up under my soapy fingers. "What the hell are you doing?" he asked when I reached around and grabbed one of his nuts.

I told him I was just having fun. "Buddy, those are *my* nuts!" He tried to jerk away from me, but he must have known that he couldn't. I really had him by one of his cahoonies. When I finally let go, turned around and faced him, he could see that I was fully erect. Although I certainly wasn't as long as he was, I am proud to say I was *fatter*. My plug started throbbing.

"Listen, man, you are not going to fuck me!" he said emphatically. There was a note of threat in his voice, as if he knew what the situation was and where it could go. This started to intrigue me.

"You're right," I said softly. I began to stroke his cock with my soapy fingers. "I won't do anything you don't want."

He looked up at me with a mixture of blankness and uncertainty. Then I saw something go through his eyes. It was the reflection of Diego, one of the Mexican farm workers, approaching us. They were migrant workers, and many of them, I admit, were hunks. They were treated badly by the owners of the farms and ranches in the area, but they managed to keep a proud streak through them. *Machismo*—attitude—call it what you will. I just knew that that streak would not look well on what I wanted to do with Works. And Works knew it, too.

He instinctively crouched down into the water and I crouched down with him, not letting go of his dick. In fact, I had one hand on his testicles and one on his peter. And I will swear before any saint—or sinner—under Heaven, that his dick was getting harder down there in the dark water. His testicles felt warm, relaxed, almost gooey, in his long, loose ball-sack.

"Hey, *muchachos*!" Diego called at us, and approached.

"Oh, no ..." Works said. "If he knows what we're doin'," he whispered to me with fear in his voice, "all hell's gonna break loose. They don't go for this kind of shit. They don't think"—he paused for a second—"men should do this with each other."

Works pretended to lie back, then sank his butt deeper into the canal, and I released his hose and the jewels under it. "Diego? Hey, you finished counting all them bushels of 'cots? Your tools put away?"

"Sure, boss!" His face hit the dirt, as if he knew it would be a good idea where not to look. Then he turned quickly, and started hustling down the dirt road to the big barn where the bushel baskets of apricots were stored before the canning trucks took them off.

I could tell there had been a funny ring in Diego's voice, as if he knew Works was only trying to get rid of him. I'd forgotten that there were certain things men weren't supposed to do, and they weren't supposed to have privacy, either, if they started doing it. Works looked at me. His eyes lowered, like he could finally relax. But just for a second. "Let's get outta here," he said, when Diego had disappeared into the distant dust. "If he saw anything, my ass is grass."

We both got out of the irrigation canal. Works put on his jeans over his sopping body. It was so hot jeans could dry directly on you. Works didn't put anything on his tanned, lean chest. It was matted with thick, black hair across his pecs. His stomach was almost hairless. The pattern of hair and smooth on his body was nice. Satisfying. I could watch it, let me tell you, for a long time, if I was only into watching Works. Suddenly he looked over at me, and a smile rolled up his face. His thin lips parted, revealing his large, very horse-like teeth. "You gave me quite a surprise," he said.

I nodded and then got into my jeans. They didn't feel good. They felt cold and clammy. I had a hard time cramming my male utensils into them, since I was still in a fairly excited state. We barefooted it over to the bunkhouse, which, I am glad to say, was empty.

It was always dark in there to keep the heat out. I noticed that Works now seemed nervous and hot. Maybe it was a combination of anxiety and horniness, too. Perspiration came off his face. We walked to the back of the bunkhouse, farthest from the door. He started to bend over a bit to get his jeans off; they slid easily off. Then he stood next to me, really shy, like he was going to ask me a personal question. But he was buck-naked, with his long pecker, semi-hard, aimed at my mouth. I sat on the edge of one of the narrow beds and tried to squeeze my jeans down over my extremely stiff dick. This was no easy matter with so much distraction—like Works' hot body—around me.

Finally, after my jeans lay in a sloppy mess at my feet, I got down on my

13

knees and took Works' full cock into my mouth. He was very hard now, and I was enjoying the hell out of it. I pulled his body closer to me so that I could smell the soap and irrigation water, all mixed with his fresh crotch smell. He pushed his hands through my hair and in about ten strokes of my mouth his jism was running down my throat. Some of it spilled off my chin and landed on my own cock. My heart pounded. In a second I was going to blast off myself, no matter what I did with my dick. I was that hot, and believe me, I could see the headlines from that, also: *San Francisco Man, Now Ranch Worker, Explodes from Spontaneous Combustion. Explains 'My Dick Got Too Hot!'*

But I didn't have a chance to do anything before Works pulled his jeans back up and walked away. Casually. Like we'd just been sitting there, chawin' about the weather or something. He was still barefoot and bare-chested. His stomach glistened from sweat. It glistened like dark, freshly oiled floorboards. His black chest hairs sparkled. His tits were like little brown coffee berries and I wanted to bite on them, but he was already by the door. He turned sharply to me. "Listen," he said, with a real warning in his voice. "Don't tell Durrance about any of this. For your own sake. Okay?" The screen door snapped open. He was gone.

He literally took my breath away—that is, if I had any breath left. I was too hot for breath. I went into the narrow craphouse at the end of the building, shut the door, and jerked off all over the toilet seat. I decided to leave it there. *That* would give the workers something to talk about. I ran some water from the small sink through my hair and counted to twenty to try to calm down. Back at my bunk, closer to the door, I pulled a fresh tee shirt out of my locker. I put on my sneakers and felt better.

The front of the bunkhouse was still empty a few minutes later, when Durrance, streaked with dust and very hot, stomped in.

"See Works?" he asked. I was still sitting at my bunk; I told him no. "He sure looked funny. What got into him? I thought you and him was over at the canal to wash. Nice evening for it, ain't it? I'm goin' over there now." Suddenly he smirked. "You want another bath?"

Durrance was about thirty-five, a few years older than Works. He was shorter and heavier than Works, but no bad looker. He had a bull neck and a thick but hard gut. But what really got you about Durrance were his eyes. They were blue and clear like a western sky. And they twinkled when he smiled. I was sure that in the right circumstances, you'd do anything for a twinkle from Durrance's eyes.

But I figured safer was a lot better than sorry. I told him no. "Sure?" he asked, all killer smile. But I knew better. If Works didn't want me to mention any of this to Durrance, there had to be a good reason. I knew under that twinkle and the dimples in his cheeks, Durrance had a nasty temper.

Everyone kept just a bit of distance from him, especially when he got into one of his moods. When he was in one, you knew it. In my week at the ranch, I saw him pound the hood of a car once with the side of his hand. He made a complete dent in it. The Mexican workers, who liked Señor Works, kept their distance from Durrance.

Both Durrance and Works had come down to Modesto from Montana, and landed jobs at "Modesto Deluxe Produce," specializing in apricots, almonds, and celery. Durrance called the place "Rancho Dingo." He was a hot mechanic. He could take a tractor apart in three-quarters of an hour, and then put it back together. He was proud of the fact that he was not stupid, in a world of a lot of stupid men. I remembered Works' warning once more, and told Durrance I was hungry, getting ready to chow, in the main building about a ten minute walk from the bunkhouse.

Durrance nodded his head. "Okay, no swim with me, right?"

I smiled.

"How long you figure you're gonna be here?" he asked me.

I leaned my head back. I felt like I'd already been at Rancho Dingo forever, but I'd been there exactly a week. Jesus, what a week—what a different world! I gibbered something about "as long as I hold out," and Durrance smiled once more—that twinkle that just looked right into you— and left. I started to feel queasy. I went back to my bunk, and stretched out for a moment. I realized Works and Durrance thought I was a cream puff. I *was* from San Francisco, which might have been half-way through the Milky Way away. I don't think either of them had ever even been into San Francisco. Then I had this real paranoid thought: Suppose Works let any of what happened in the canal, and later in the bunkhouse, out? I knew my nuts had got the worst of me. Suppose Diego just let it leak to the other migrants that he thought he saw me and the foreman doing *puto* numbers down by the ol' watering hole?

A shiver shot through me. I saw the whole thing in my mind: the Mexicans came, in some ways, from a more repressed culture. Although they lived in the bunkhouse with us, there was often tension. I wasn't sure how all of this would sit with them. One night, suppose they—well—decided to rope me to a tractor, and see how fast they could drive it with me tied to the back of it?

My nerves got the most of me. I wasn't sure I could go in for chow right then. My stomach started playing hopscotch. I thought about my past, and my distant life in San Francisco. I grew up in an absolutely uninteresting place in the middle of our nation, and at twenty-eight decided to go off to San Francisco and make it as a computer operator. I landed a job at the Bank of America, but after a year I discovered that my nine-to-five gig was really interfering with my real life: partaking in San Francisco's wonderful bar life, and getting some interesting cock when I wanted it.

So, as they say in computer lingo, my input did not interface with my Main Frame. And, after enough lame excuses from me, Main Frame fired me. No severance. No benefits. Chicken scratch unemployment.

In other words, in plain English, I was out on my ass with a heavy-weight apartment above the Castro. Bills were eating me up alive. Finally, one night in a leather bar, a very friendly guy told me about farm work out in Modesto. "It's not all Silicon Valley out there yet, and they don't give a shit about resumés."

A couple of days later, I got a computer buddy from the Bank who had just arrived in the Bay Area to write me a check for three months' rent, plus a thousand bucks to sit on my chairs and use my sheets. I'd been in good shape from working out at the gym. I was still young enough to do hard work, so I figured why not just cast my ass out on the next bus for Modesto and see what pops up?

The first day I arrived in Modesto, I met Works at the counter of a coffee shop. I'm not sure how it happened, but we smiled at each other. He looked at me and said, "I can take you back to Modesto Deluxe in my truck, put you to work, or you can stay in town and see if a better offer comes along."

I asked him where his pickup was—he could have picked me up right then—and he said outside. I couldn't believe how fast it all happened, or that I had screwed it up so quickly by putting the moves on him.

I was still feeling pretty low when Durrance came back in from the irri-gation canal. He walked past without even nodding to me. This did not appear to me to be a good sign. Since his bunk was close to mine, he stripped down to a heavy but work-hard ass, and then put on some fresh work pants and a clean denim shirt that showed off his chest. "What's wrong? Ain't chowin'?"

I told him I really wasn't all that hungry. He nodded a bit to me, serious-ly, without his usual twinkle, and left for the chow hall.

A few minutes later, the sun was almost down, except for a ribbon of purple light at the horizon. It was darker and cooler. I left my bunk and walked outside.

Suddenly, I genuinely liked being there. I didn't want to go back to *the* Bank, or any fucking bank, for that matter. Ever again. I climbed up to a place above the field we'd been refencing and watched the whole landscape pour out from under me. I felt like dancing. The stars were coming out, and they were bigger and more beautiful than anything in any disco in San Francisco. I felt so happy, as if perhaps I could find myself out here in some way. I thought about the life I'd led in San Francisco, the bars and the one-night stands with guys who never really became your friends. There had to be something else in my life than that, although to tell you the truth, I wasn't sure where to find it. But being out here with rows and rows of fruit trees and the celery planted the way it was—in perfect, beautiful lines—made me feel good about myself. I stopped feeling anxious and returned to the bunkhouse, got into my bunk, and fell asleep.

I was awakened—I'm not sure when, but later—by a hand pressed firmly over my mouth. "Get him!" Durrance ordered, and he held me down while Works grabbed my feet and flipped me out of the bed. I looked up at Works, but he wouldn't return my look. He kept turning away from me, and every time he did, it was like being stabbed. I knew he was disgusted with me. I wasn't wearing a stitch of clothes, and I felt—unusual for me—embarrassed at being naked.

Durrance grabbed my hair, and whispered into my ear, "Now, you make any noise, friend, and every Mexican from here to the Border is gonna wake up and I don't think they like people like you."

His logic was pretty convincing. No, I didn't protest. They threw a sheet over me, and dragged me out to the same beautiful fields I'd been in before, by the irrigation canal. Durrance spread the sheet on the ground, and the two of them shucked off their jeans and work boots. They both kept their denim work shirts on. Durrance had a thick, stubby hard-on and he aimed it at my face. He was uncut and skin still covered the head. "I heard you like to suck dick," he said and forced my mouth open with his left hand, sticking his fingers into it. His hand tasted like slightly salty leather. His nails were ground down short; they tasted of heavy-grade lube oil.

He stuffed his cock into my mouth. "I heard you made advances to my friend," he growled, and began to fuck my face.

"Durrance!" Works said. "He didn't make no advances to me. I mean ... I coulda got away from him."

"Shut up, bean-brain," Durrance cut in, then pulled his cock out of my mouth. I felt dazed, really numb, like I wasn't sure any of this was happening. It could have been a dream; maybe I was still asleep in my bunk. Maybe I was still asleep in San Francisco.

I looked up at them, and wondered what was going to happen next. Then I heard some loud noises coming from the other side of the bunkhouse. Flashlights came out. God, I thought, they're all coming to get me.

My eyes watered. That happened when I was under a lot of stress. But I could see that Works looked concerned. "Those Mexicans aren't coming here, are they?" he asked. "Durrance! I told you not to tell 'em. *Shit!*"

Durrance's face became one big smirk. "Yeh," he answered. He had that smile again. It was wicked. All cold blue eyes. You could have frozen meat with those eyes. "They're comin' over here to watch!"

"You ... you promised, Durrance!"

"Nah, Works. Don't worry. I was joshin'. Diego's just going into town with some of the boys. They're gonna get *some*. Know what I mean?"

Works looked relieved. Frankly, I felt better myself. Then Durrance turned around from me. His hard, naked butt poked out from under his denim shirt and glowed in the half-light of the moon. "Now, I'm gonna get *me* some," he said, and he went over to his jeans and pulled out a tube of petroleum jelly from his jeans' pocket. I knew he used that on his hands for engine burns.

"I'm gonna grease up my dick and fuck you like a pig," he said to me.

Works turned away in disgust. He looked even more naked with his shirt on and his pecker hanging down limply. "Durrance, why don't you leave him alone? Make him blow you, but don't fuck him. That's ... not right."

"Yeh, Works, *you* tell me what's not right!" He got down close to my ear and ordered, "Boy, you get on your stomach real fast!"

I knew I had to do what he said. Then I felt Durrance's weight on top of me, and he was pushing his fat dick through my tight ass. When I got nervous, my muscles clammed up. "You gonna let me in there?" he asked. "Or are we gonna have to work you over?"

I didn't have a chance to answer. Works started to jam his feet back into his jeans. "Durrance, I ain't doing anything. This here is not right." He started to walk off in his bare feet, carrying his boots to the bunkhouse.

"Works ... oh, shit, Works...!" Durrance called after him.

Works suddenly turned around. "Durrance, what the hell do you want me to do? I ain't gonna rape him. That's not right."

Durrance pulled his dick out of me. It hurt. He'd been rough. "Shit, Works!" He suddenly sat up on his knees. "Works, you know I couldn't hurt him if you didn't want me to." He looked down at me. "Damn, it's okay, it's gonna be okay," he said softly. His attitude changed so fast I was shocked.

He squatted down on his haunches closer to my face, and then started to stroke my hair. He ran his greasy fingers over my cheeks and down my lips. "It was just fun. We was just havin' fun. Shit! I can't do anything Works don't want."

For a moment, I thought my heart was going to stop. These two cowboys had really scared the living hell out of me. But now they seemed very different. "Let me show you nice," Durrance said. His hard, slightly stubbly face came closer to mine. I could smell his cool breath, and the slight whiff of Vitalis on his hair. He put his mouth softly on my face, and then his thick fingers found my soft, very frightened cock. They warmed me, and I started—whether I wanted to or not—to stiffen. "We was just gonna scare you," Durrance admitted. Works smiled, and he shuffled back over. A breeze stirred up again. It seemed for a while that the air around me had gone dead hot. Suddenly Works dropped his boots, and unbuttoned his shirt and let his jeans drop in the dust. He took his long, skinny cock in his hand. It was more than half hard. The thick head was getting full.

"We done stuff like this before with other guys," Works confessed. He brought his cock close to me, and I took it into my hand and knew that I wanted it back in my mouth again. He must have known what I wanted. "I gotta admit, Durrance gets real jealous."

Durrance smiled sheepishly, then went down with his mouth on my dick. He and Works played with each other's bodies. They got excited and started panting. I watched them for a moment, and also saw the moonlight skimming off the irrigation canal. It made the water in it seem transparent. Now I felt I could really breathe there at Rancho Dingo, and I let both of them fuck me.

THE COLD

2

The second week after I arrived in the camp in the Adirondacks, the cold set in. The camp belonged to my friend Mike in New York—actually to his parents who were away in Florida—and Mike loaned it to me because he knew I was burned out with the city and I needed a place that was quiet. This was quiet. You could hear every one of your thoughts. Sometimes I thought you could even hear the blood working its way into your finger tips. The blood made a noise like a small hole in an air hose: pss-pss-pss. It was that quiet in the camp, even during the day.

The camp was near Malone, New York, about a spit away from the Canadian border. There were several Indian settlements around there, and when I took the Jeep over to the General Store eight miles down the road, I'd see Indians come in. They were friendly, but kept a distance from you, and they didn't seem to notice the cold the way I did. It was mid-November, a pretty dicey time, Mike warned me, when one day you could walk outside in shirt sleeves and the next morning go out and feel the snot in your nose freeze and drop right under you. I complained about the cold to Pete, the French Canadian, and his wife Genevieve, who ran the store, but the Indians never bellyached about it. They seemed to me to be a silent group. They got what they wanted and left. Usually whites hardly said anything to the Indians, and I—out of a certain shyness—gave them an accept able amount of distance and did the same.

The first day the real cold set in, I got kind of spooked by it, which was probably natural, being alone in this place—one of the coldest corners of America—in a cabin with no running water and no electricity. I did have a good wood burning stove and enough wood in the shed attached to keep me warm indefinitely. There was also a generous supply of canned "staples," like deviled ham, peas-and-carrots, and Campbell's Soups, and with the Jeep Mike had lent me, all I had to do was get in it and go down to the store for anything else I needed.

I'd never driven a Jeep before and I was a bit daunted by it. I'd lived in Manhattan long enough almost to forget how to put the key in and work the clutch. But it all came back quickly enough, and I soon learned how to get the damn thing going, although reverse still wasn't easy. Luckily, everything around the camp seemed to be either uphill or downhill, with little in reverse. There was almost no traffic on the roads, but a few people in their pickup trucks waved at me. I enjoyed this sort of friendliness. It was brief and not very personal, but it made me feel that I wasn't totally out of my skull here. There were a few others like me and there was something kind of daring about spending the winter in this part of the mountains. I'm sure people figured that if I was fool enough to spend the winter here, I was good enough to wave to. No questions asked.

But the Indians that I saw never waved, and after a while I started to get skittish about them.

Or maybe I was just skittish about the cold. Mike had warned me about that. Cabin fever was real in a long, hard winter. "If it gets too much for you—being alone and all—then just say fuck it and take the Jeep back to Malone and get a train back. Leave the Jeep at my parents' house and I'll pick it up in May."

To tell you the truth, I hadn't really understood then what he was talking about. But the cold came in so sharply and so suddenly that it was like being slapped about by a huge, faceless giant. It seemed to menace me, follow me even into the cabin, and become an enemy. Everything got harder to do. Everything took more energy than I thought it would. Even sleeping seemed to take more energy. Getting into one of the cabin's two narrow, hard, cold twin beds; wrapping two Army blankets tightly around me, mummy fashion; waiting for the bed to warm up enough from my own body heat—none of that made hitting the sack alone each night inviting.

But sleeping was a way to conserve energy, so I started sleeping during the day—usually after I'd poured a half shot of whiskey into my tea to keep warm. The warm, boozy tea was a great sleep bringer.

But then at night, when I really wanted to sleep, I couldn't. Thoughts raced through me. I'd start to think about all the people I knew back in New York. I would see their faces. My own loneliness would start to hit me; really pinch me hard.

Somewhere in this procession of faces, I'd see Clark. He was this younger, twerpy guy I'd been—you know, I really hate to admit this! Okay, I'd been in love with him. It was hard for me to believe I'd actually been in love with this guy, and he'd occupied so much of my thoughts. But I had been—and when I started to think about him, I'd start to beat off. I'd grab my dick at the base, just above my warm, slightly furry balls, as my cock started to get stiff.

I noticed that in the warm bed, under the blankets—but with the cold air in the cabin—if I grabbed my cock just a bit harder (and I *will* admit that I have big balls), even the hairs on my ball sack would feel prickly. Like there was electricity running through them. The hairs would stand up and salute a bit, and everything around my genitals, including me, would get hotter. I'd feel the warmth flowing through me. The warmth from the tea, the whiskey, the creaky bed, and the cast iron stove that had a way of going out and leaving the cabin like a refrigerator.

That warmth would make me think even more about Clark—this skinny, "sensitive" young man (who was always telling me how insensitive I was)—who worked in a bank and wore snappy little ties that he bought on sale at Brooks Brothers. I'd think, for an instance, about his suits and his ties, but mostly I thought about him in the middle of hot sex, with his business clothes scattered all over my apartment. He had fine, pale skin and small teeth. Long fingers and long toes. Of course I thought about his lips, and his nice, small mouth. His smooth, narrow chest and boyish body; skinny hips and legs—and his hard, skinny cock that always seemed so much longer than I expected it to be, with its really sensitive, large head.

I thought a lot about the head of his cock. I liked the head of his cock a lot more than I liked his head. He was spacey and dizzy, but his cock—it was a wonder. Sometimes it didn't even seem like a part of him. It was separate. I could play with it for hours, even while he read a book. Or was he just pretending to read?

The fact that he was such a little banker straight-arrow and I was such a fuck-up probably kept us going. It added just the right amount of tension and interest to what we had between us. So maybe he was only pretending to read. Maybe it was just a game, while I played with his dick. But even thinking about his cock made being in that cabin warmer and more bearable. His cock would get me going, running my fingers over my own shaft, working myself out of my coldness. My loneliness.

Boy, did I want Clark to be there—just then—and I wanted the head of his dick in my mouth.

23

But after I'd made a whole handful of jism, after it had spurted fresh out of my dick and I was trying like hell to figure out what to do with it (Mental Note: buy Kleenex at General Store), I was glad Clark wasn't there.

Then I would have had to hear about his yuppie job at the fucking bank, and I didn't want to hear about that.

Sometimes I thought about ingesting my own cum. I know, you're thinking this is a sick story, but if you've ever been stuck some place where there's nothing around you but cold—anyway, two days with Clark and I know I would have ended up chasing him around the cabin with the wood ax just to shut him up.

When you're alone, you start to think about really basic things and I wondered how I'd *ever* fallen for someone like Clark, and how useless love was, really, and then—strangely enough—I started to miss it. I started to miss love the way you can miss good food or real warmth in the midst of the coming of too much cold. Then I started to think about the Indians and the trees.

Somewhere out there in the middle of all those hardwood trees, there had to be a young, hot Indian who was looking for male companionship of a more interesting nature than you usually got at the General Store. This became quite a fantasy of mine, and I'd hitch a ride on it and start to see him: his dark eyes flashing between the bare trees. Thick, black hair glistening in the moonlight. Broad shoulders. Huge hands and feet. I would meet him and we'd follow each other deeper into the woods, then we'd both get naked very quickly. We'd end up greasing each other with bear fat—the type Pete sold that you could use for almost anything—I could imagine myself sucking at his tits, his navel, his fat balls. We'd be so hot and ready for pleasure that the cold would never bother us.

I jerked off an awful lot thinking about that, but every time I went out, the fantasy instantly disappeared. The Indians would keep their distance, and so would I. Often, they'd ignore me completely. Inside, I felt frozen. It was like the cold had set in between me and the world. Then, when I left Pete's and I got back into my Jeep, I'd realize how lonely I'd be back at the camp. By the time I unloaded the groceries and stoked up the fire, and had my tea with whiskey, all I wanted to do was jerk off again—while Clark and my Indians came back to see me—and then I just wanted to fall asleep to block out the loneliness and the cold.

24

Then suddenly, into my second week there in the cold, I started to enjoy things. That sense of drifting in time—sleeping when I wanted to, drinking whenever I damn well felt like it, the silence, the wild nature around me—I started to like all of that. But the thing that still bothered me was being alone at night—especially when there were no moon or stars out and the blackness outside the camp overwhelmed me. Then I started feeling like I wasn't just drifting along in nature, but I was being swallowed up by it. Isolated animal sounds, like the shrieking of a loon or the deer ambling through the woods—sounds from probably half a mile away—would shake the hell out of me.

I had two nights just like that, and on the third, I was wired to the teeth. I swigged a good bit of the fifth of cheap Canadian blended whiskey Pete had sold me at the store, ate some Campbell's chicken noodle soup and a half a loaf of stale white bread, and then I stripped down to bare skin to go to sleep.

The bed eventually got warm, after I'd settled into it. A small fire was going in the cast iron stove and I figured it would continue for most of the night. I closed my eyes, and told myself that I had to drift off. Then I realized I wasn't going to be able to sleep again. It wasn't just that I was seeing old faces from New York. There were no animal noises this time; but something was definitely keeping me awake.

I got up, bare-assed and barefooted, and stalked up to the window near the bed. There I saw the first snow since I'd arrived coming down. I felt some relief. Finally, this was a good sign. "Ees too cold t' snow," Pete had been telling me for a week. Now, I started to look forward to next day.

I remained stark naked, and got myself some more whiskey and put it into what was left of the lukewarm tea, and then carried the cup back to bed with me. I started thinking about the Jeep. I hoped it would be alright out in the snow. Mike had warned me that sometimes you got a drift that could literally lock the Jeep in.

I decided not to worry. I actually began to loosen up a bit, and felt my muscles and mind relax as my body warmed up inside and out. I drank some more of the tea, then something happened that tightened every nerve in me.

It was a sound like deep crunching coming from outside. It was distant at first, like it was coming from the narrow tractor trail off the main road that led to the camp. I hadn't been expecting anyone. No one knew I was there, except Mike and his parents.

The sound got louder and deeper. Suddenly I realized that I was going to have visitors.

I couldn't see anything further than a few feet from the cabin, because of the snow and the darkness. I made sure all the lights were out in the cabin, and I waited. I realized how vulnerable I was ... suppose there was someone, or a group of whatever out there: hoods, creeps, punks, lost serial murderers (???)—my worst fantasies started to take over. I could see them just *drifting* along, like I had been in the cold, robbing summer cabins. Doing anything they wanted to do.

Mike had warned me that vandalism was a problem. That was why his parents had been happy to have me stay there. But suppose this didn't stop at vandalism? Suppose they weren't going to stop. What was I going to do?

I knew I couldn't just wait naked for the worst to happen. It wasn't in me. I had to weigh the situation in my mind. I wondered if I should just go out there and meet whomever it was—let them know *immediately* I was there, and that I wasn't just someone to fuck with. My eyes ran around the dark cabin. There was the heavy wood ax lying in front, near the door. I knew I could grab it, just to let them know that I was ready to use it.

I padded over, quietly, and got the ax. Then I brought it back to the freezing window, and crouched down as far as I could. I waited to see what was going to happen next.

Out of the thick snow, another Jeep pulled up beside mine. Then a large man, fully dressed for winter in boots and a parka, got out by himself. I saw that he was carrying a rifle. He walked slowly, carefully, over to the cabin. The snow started to blow in even heavier. I saw that it had already half covered Mike's Jeep, and it would soon do the same for the one that had just parked.

Then it dawned on me: this guy could easily figure out that Mike's cabin wasn't empty. Even with the ax gripped in my hand, I became scared. An ax was no match for a rifle. I eased myself quietly into my jeans, managed to buckle my belt, and then went over to the door and made very sure that it was bolted from inside. My heart was pounding; I wondered what the hell I was going to do next. I looked around in the dark, then hurried to the table and grabbed a large butcher knife and put it inside the top of my right work boot. I put on my socks, laced up the boots, and threw on a flannel shirt.

There was a loud knock on the door. I waited.

"Mike?" a deep voice called.

I exhaled, purely relieved. I unbolted and opened the door. He was already covered in snow and looked blue-chilled even in the dark. I asked him in, although there as no light in the cabin.

"You must've been asleep, Mike. I'm sorry I woke you," he said, as he lumbered in to the dark cabin.

I told him I wasn't Mike, and lit a kerosene lamp and then took a look at him. He went back over to the door, put his rifle up, and told me that his name was Rich Barnsworth. He was an old high school buddy of Mike's. He knew Mike's family had the camp, so he stopped by—he came out this way for the beginning of hunting season. He spoke slowly, measuring his words. Legally, he said, he could shoot one elk, if he found one. His family used a hunting camp twenty miles away, and he was on his way to it, but he hadn't figured on so much snow coming down that night.

"When I saw the Jeep, I knew somebody had to be home," he said. He was certainly a large, almost hulking guy, about thirty-two, with lots of thick, dark, silky hair on his head. His hair was shiny—really beautiful—and it reminded me of the Indians I'd seen at the store. He had high cheekbones, but he also had a heavy winter beard, something the Indians never seemed to have. His beard was coal black, with just a few stray gray hairs at the sides. I noticed that his beard was also silky, and glowed like the freshly brushed coat of an Irish setter. It wasn't crinkly or curly.

"I didn't realize you'd be asleep so early," he said to me, without really looking at my boots. He told me he didn't have to stay, he could go. He didn't want to be a bother. I told him no, that I was very happy to have some company. It was just—I was embarrassed to have to confess this—I wasn't used to being alone in the woods.

"You're from New York?" I told him I was, and he confessed to me that the City scared him more than anything in the woods. I offered him some tea, and he took his coat off and slowly sat down. I was sure his body must have been stiff and creaky from the cold. I opened up another can of Campbell's Soup—this time split pea—poured some water from the water bucket into my soup pot, and put it on top of the cast iron stove.

"That's a good stove," he told me, and he showed me how to control the damper to get even more heat out of it. I was sitting close to the stove, and when he walked over to me, and then bent down next to me, I noticed that he did move slowly, as if his very largeness needed more time. I was used to crazy people in New York darting around me like little bullets. Suddenly, I knew I liked this man. I decided I definitely *didn't* want him to leave for a while.

When he finished the soup, cleaning the bowl with a piece of white bread, I took out what was left of the cheap Canadian whiskey, and we drank several cups of it, first with and then without the tea. I could tell he was relaxing. He started telling me about life in the woods. Some of the stories went back to his father and grandfather. He had lots of stories about the Indians, how smart they had once been, before everything had been taken away from them. His own family had been up by the Canadian border since the Civil War. He'd been married once, but his wife ran away with another man—who'd actually been a friend of his. He closed his eyes and told me that it had all happened right under his nose. Now he lived alone a lot, and had little to do with most people, except his large family that was scattered all over these parts.

I got up my courage. "You look part Indian," I said to him. He smiled at me, and nodded his head. He poured some more of the Canadian whiskey and told me that his great grandmother had been an Indian, and so had his ex-wife.

His telling me this seemed to do something for me. I found myself getting looser than I'd been in ages. My coldness and loneliness started to melt away, and with them so did many of the uptight fears I brought with me from New York. Now I found it hard to control myself. His revelations stirred the desires in me—desires to be physically close to him. I wanted him badly. His dark, black eyes kept looking at me, as if he, too, wanted to ask a question that he couldn't.

Suddenly, we stopped talking and I felt a blast of coldness enter the room.

"I think I'm gonna have to go," he said to me. He got up very slowly. He didn't even look back at me, and now I knew that I wanted him so badly that I felt suddenly like I was drowning as he was leaving me. I jumped up and grabbed his arm.

"No!" I said—the word shot right out of me. "I mean, you shouldn't leave now, Rich. We had a lot to drink, and you might get lost out there."

He bit his bottom lip. "It's okay. I know these woods. I know the way in my sleep." He smiled at me, and I realized that I had to do something, right there.

I made up a story about my Jeep. I wasn't sure if it'd still run after so much snow, and I might need somebody to help me with it. He wasn't going to just let this dumb New Yorker freeze in the snow, was he?

He smiled again nervously. "Listen," he said, not looking at me at all. "I don't know if I want to spend the night here." He got up, and slowly put on his big parka.

I looked away from him. I felt very rejected. Hurt. It was a feeling like being slapped, like when the beautiful music inside you stops. Was it that obvious how much I wanted him? I felt that no matter how casual I tried to be, he could see right through me. I'd heard that the cold did strange things to people; perhaps he knew that already. He knew that loneliness would drive me to him, just as straight as desire would.

The door parted. Snow came in for a second, then he left and shut it behind him. No goodbye. Just gone. I swallowed my pain, and then ran after him. Ran—no coat—I would have gone barefoot. I ran up to him as we approached his Jeep. "Are you SURE you can DRIVE?!!" I shouted. Snow clung to my hair and the back of my neck. It covered the air. It made the air feel warmer, but muffled everything. You couldn't hear much.

We got to his Jeep. He got in, and immediately I jumped in too, from the other side. He had his rifle between us. He turned over to me, and grabbed the rifle. His dark brow hardened. He looked tense. "What the hell are you doing?" he asked.

I felt myself let go of everything. Pride. Everything. I could barely breathe from the cold. "I don't want you to leave," I said. "I'm lonely."

He turned away, and then looked at me like he couldn't believe I'd said it. I had no idea what he'd do; what he was capable of doing. Then he smiled. The tension between us broke. He leaned over towards me so that I could smell the warm whiskey on his breath. I felt myself getting physically excited. He put his large, gloved hand on my head, and shook some of the snow out. "I understand," he whispered. He opened the door and got out of the Jeep. I had to hold myself back for a second—I was shaking from cold and nerves. He waited calmly by the Jeep, with the snow whirling around him, then I got out, and he followed me back into the cabin.

Silently, we had some more of the tea with whiskey. I felt very happy, although I still wasn't sure what was going to happen. "Would you mind if I washed up a bit?" he finally asked. I poured some of the bucket of water into a small, enamel wash basin, then I added some boiling water from the kettle to warm it.

He took off his shirt, and then I took off mine. He was built very well, with big shoulders and large, dark pecs. He had thick nipples that looked hardened from the cold. There was a good dusting of silky, black hair on his chest. It triangled smartly down his taut stomach to his navel, where it got thicker and disappeared into his jeans. I handed him a wash rag, and he began to scrub his face and neck.

I took another rag and went over my face and neck. Then I warmed it again in the water, and began to stroke the back of his neck and shoulders with it. I felt him tighten up and then relax. I stroked deeper, and washed his back completely.

I started to wash his lower back, and followed the hard lines of his back muscles to where they tapered down to a firm waist. I wanted to dig into his jeans, and stroke his ass, wash each of his firm butt cheeks, and then follow the warm wash rag with my even warmer tongue. My hands started to roam around his front and I grabbed his stomach and held onto it with one hand, while I stroked the small of his strong back, just above his butt, with the other.

Suddenly, he unbuttoned his jeans and let them drop a bit, revealing his beautiful, hairy ass. I sank down slightly and started to stroke and caress it. His butt was round and firm, musky and exciting to me. My other hand reached down in front of him. I realized he had a near hard-on, large and very thick. My hand gently rubbed the head of his circumcised cock. It was blunt and thick, swelling and getting much hotter.

I got up, without letting go of his dick, and faced him and opened my mouth and kissed him. His body suddenly tightened. He jerked away from me; I felt him reel back. The warm moment had broken. The distance between us was back there again—with the cold that now seemed to rush in from outside. There was a moment of dead, backcountry quiet.

I looked right at him. I swear I could hear him breathing.

"I'm going to need some help," he whispered to me, then he sat down again, at the table. I couldn't let myself say anything. I was too afraid, afraid he was just going to walk away. He bent over slowly and began loosening his pants. He untied his right boot, and managed to pull his right leg out of his jeans. Then he started carefully to roll down his left pants leg and when it rolled down just below his knee, I realized his left leg was artificial.

"Can you help me get this off?" he asked. "I'm a little drunk, you see, and it's hard to do this when I'm tight."

I kneeled down and helped him unbuckle the artificial leg. It seemed horribly heavy and complicated. I wasn't sure what to do with it, but he just picked it up, like it weighed almost nothing, and put it next to him by the chair. He was now sitting naked. He still looked very beautiful to me. His lower body was paler than his chest, and I was overcome with longing for him. I took the washcloth again and started to wash his muscular thighs, his right leg down to his foot, and what was left of the other leg, which was amputated a little lower than mid-calf. I brought the wash basin over so that he was warmed as much as possible by the warm water and the cloth. And every place that the wash cloth went, my own tongue followed and I had his cock, his balls, his thighs, and even the sensitive curve of the stump of his left leg in my mouth at some point.

He liked all of this. He groaned. Closed his eyes, but did not really touch me, while I licked and sucked him. But when I finished washing him, he grabbed my neck and shoulders, and leaning on me, we got into the narrow bed that I slept in. By then, I had all my clothes off, and I had to be careful with my right boot, because the butcher knife was still in it, and I didn't want him to see that.

In bed, I turned the kerosene lamp down to a needle point of light and then put my lips on his mouth again, and this time he opened his mouth up. We kissed for a long time, and then I ran my mouth down his chest, sucking on each of his hard, dark nipples, getting a lot of his silky chest hairs into my mouth.

I ran my tongue down further, licking at his navel until I reached his cock. It was fever hot and ready for me. I sucked him all the way down to his balls, and he groaned every time my mouth stroked him, but he made little effort to return any attention to me, and I started to jerk myself off while I sucked him.

Then, to my complete surprise, he looked up at me—I had my head buried between his large legs—and he said, "Do you want to fuck me?"

I'll admit, I didn't have to be convinced of this, but just accepted it as my own good fortune. He took some of his own spit to lube up his beautiful, muscled asshole. I got under him, and he sat on me. Since he had one leg less, he was much lighter. He grabbed my waist and for the first time really let go of himself. He became totally wild every time I pumped my cock into

30

him—tearing at me, ramming his tongue into my mouth, holding me, while I bucked into him.

I was on the verge of coming, but I kept trying to hold back. He must have known this because he let go of me, and fell back on the bed, so that I could fuck him and work his cock with my hands at the same time. As we got closer and closer, I became totally uncontrollable and started grabbing, licking, even biting the sensitive stump of his left leg. I rolled my tongue around it, and watched his face register complete happiness, while I knew I was as excited by this as he was.

To hold on even more, I pulled out some, and we lay there for a moment, on the brink of complete release. It was hard to believe this man was a stranger, some one I had feared hardly more than an hour earlier. Now the silence between us seemed beautiful, the closeness wonderful. I listened. I could hear him breathing under his lush, silky beard, and I could hear the snow come down on the roof, and even the stars move above me. I kissed him some more, then edged my cock even deeper into him, so that I could pull him closer to me. I began wildly sucking his chest, his nipples, his neck and mouth—every part of him I could reach while fucking him. Then, as I could not hold back a second longer, I exploded inside of him—and as soon as I did, I took his fat, hard dick into my mouth, and sucked him off completely.

We lay for a moment on the bed, limper than the used wash rags. I had no idea what I would say to him, but he broke the silence. "I wasn't sure I could spend the night with you," he said, looking directly into my face with his soft eyes. "I feel so funny about having this bad leg. It's like I don't want to tell people about it, but I always feel that they know there's something strange about me. A lot of people get scared off. I lost it after a hunting accident out here. I was alone then, like you."

I pulled him closer to me and kissed him some more. I couldn't keep my hands away from his silky, Indian hair. Or his beard, or the hair on his chest. A few minutes later, he fell asleep or passed out. I couldn't sleep, but got out of bed and went over to the window. The snow had finally stopped and the moon—three-quarters full—came out. The light bouncing off the snow was sharp and clear. Soon, I knew, it would get even colder. I remembered that the cold had once scared everything out of me, but now I felt there was less to be scared of, and I couldn't wait to get back into bed with him.

$\int$EX $\int$TICK

Hans, the German able-bodied seaman, approached from around the corner. I wondered what he was doing down there. It was as dark as a cave down in the second storage hold where I was working, and by orders he was supposed to be up front, scraping and painting the foredeck on the second shift. Hans was a looker. Your eyes, without any effort, could stick to him. First of all, he was built like a brick shithouse. He was all hard muscle and had thick, powerful biceps and forearms that weren't just for show but for real work. He had a thick neck and corn-silk white hair. He looked like a pale, blond bull. As he approached me, I thought about his small, blue eyes. There was something quick and sexy about them, like they were taking in everything. As if they did more than simply see, but felt as well. I was sure Hans' eyes had to be to his brain what a warm tongue was to a mouth. His eyes tasted as well as saw.

But then, I couldn't even see his eyes. It was too dark, and I was supposed to be jotting down the stock numbers of barrels of naval stores in my manifest. Each barrel of this goo had a number with something like twelve digits in it. Part of the number showed where it came from and the date it was moved to our ship. I had to connect all these numbers, make some kind of pattern out of them, and then feed them into the ship's computer. It was a boring job, and I didn't let it take my mind off Hans for a second.

I remembered the way his eyes looked at me across the table in the seamen's mess. I sat across from him a lot. The ship had two messes—seamen's and officers. Occasionally, passengers came aboard—usually trying to find a cheap ride between places like Pago Pago and Bora Bora. The freighter was not equipped for passengers; no pool, no dance band. But they did get to eat with the officers, a repressed, stuffy bunch. Their food wasn't any better than ours, but their mess was quieter. The seamen were loud. So loud that if my eyes drifted over to Hans and just stayed there, nobody noticed. Being in the merchant marine is about nine-tenths boring and the other tenth worth all the hours of sitting with your thumb up your butt. Believe me, I'd been waiting for this other tenth to pop up for a couple of weeks.

That is, to be precise, I kept expecting at least one—and hopefully some—of the guys who worked on this tub to come on to me. I was getting tired of just jerking off down below deck in my cabin. I'd signed on with the boat because I knew one other guy, Casey, who was also gay and was a cook's assistant. Casey was short and in his forties and very quick witted. "You gotta be a little more forward," he said to me. Casey had grown up in Pittsburgh, but had an accent that was kind of half Irish and half all over. He was great at filching booze out of the locked steward's cabin. The steward, who was a horse's ass, had caught Casey once with a half bottle of Drambuie. Casey just said it was for the chief engineer, whom I have a feeling was secretly a brother of ours—if you know what I mean. Casey could steal, but would never snitch. I had tried to psych him out about Hans and all he'd say was "Nuthin' ventured, nuthin' gained!"

You had to be very cool out there on a boat. It wasn't so much that people would nail your ass if they found out you were queer. It was that there was a lot of resentment about 'special relationships.' Of course, I'm not saying that you'd never run into boat-bound psycho cases who might try to murder you if they suspected something gay about you—there are bad people on dry land, too. But out in the middle of the Pacific, you can't run away from them, so it's a good idea to keep your hands to yourself. But this Hans character was starting to seep into my dry dreams, not to mention a couple of wet ones.

Just the *thought* of his hot body could get my dick hard. And the sight of it—wow! I ran into him once in the shower. He's over six feet with one of these great German butts, solid, from lifting barrels with his legs. On the boat, you learn quickly to lift with your legs, and that made his butt look great. I would say he was about thirty—close to my age—and he was generally very quiet. My knowledge of German is limited to "Guten Tag," but I don't think that was what held us back. See, there were five other Germans on board—including the ship's cook, whom Casey swore was trying to poison us ("A German cook," he said, "is like a tone-deaf musician. The Germans fry an egg for an hour!"). I noticed that Hans didn't talk much to them, either.

Besides the six Germans, there were a couple of hot South Americans, who never seemed to be around when you wanted them. The rest were Americans, although the freighter, for tax reasons, was not registered as American. The boat was registered in Monaco, which gave this sleazy barge a kind of romance. I loved telling friends that my working address was care of the Principality of Monaco. I had as little to do with the Americans as I could. I had joined the merchant marine to get away, and I didn't want to be one of those Americans who dragged America, along with the shopping malls and Golden Arches, with them wherever they went.

I'm not sure if that was exactly why I was drawn to Hans, but it seemed as good a reason as any. "Hey—Hans!" I shouted to him, and shined my flashlight over to his direction. "*Guten Tag!*" His small eyes, almost hidden behind his cheekbones, lit up, like little metallic points of blue. I liked those crisp, blue eyes. I really did. He flashed a great smile at me.

"*Ist das* you here?" he winked. "I think you down here *schlaffen.*"

If only, I thought to myself, I was *schlaffen*, and *with* him.

"No," I said. "I'm not sleeping. Just working."

"*Das ist nicht gut*," he said, and winked again. "All verk and no play is no good." He pushed his large hands across his massive chest so that his tee shirt pulled away from his pants, clearing his taut belly. Now I sincerely wished he hadn't done that. The thought of his stomach, with just the smallest mouthful of fat on it, laced all over with fine, blond, German hairs, got to me. If he was playing with me, he was now pouring gasoline on my fire. I wanted to eat his dick right then. But I knew I'd better hold back. One thing was really certain: you could get into a lot of trouble on a tight ship like this one, loaded with Rotarian-type American officers who never seemed to have enough paper work to do. I could see the First Mate right now seriously explaining to me how this "breach of morals" would cause him to dump my ass out on the first port. That would mean hitching back to the States from somewhere in Goa on the next boat, and there was no telling what kind of garbage float that could be.

"*Viel Arbeit?*" Hans said, sympathetically getting closer to me. Suddenly, his heavy hand went up playfully to my chin. He ran his hand through my hair. He was driving me nuts.

I took a deep breath. "Yeh, hard work," I said. That much German I knew. I tried to think straight ahead. I counted backwards from five, so that the stiffening in my crotch slowed down. Then I explained slowly to Hans that I had this work to do. The completed manifest had to be ready by nine the next morning. It was already 7 pm. Nineteen hundred hours. "I'm afraid

I'm going to have to be down here half the night," I said.

"Captain, he son-of-bitch," Hans said. I agreed. The Captain was actually a Harvard man. He kept thinking this was the H.M.S. Pinafore. I smiled and asked Hans why he was down in the second hold, and not up. He told me it was getting too cold up on the deck, which I was sure it was. This part of the Pacific, roughly two hundred miles out from from the southern coast of Chile, near Concepción, started to dip very cold in August, as soon as the sun went down.

"Too cold up there?" I said, looking into his eyes with the flashlight on.

He nodded his head.

I decided then I had to do something. Okay, I'd throw a bit of caution to the wind. I told him I was really glad he was down there. I told him I was happy to see him.

He looked at me as if he didn't quite know what to do with the words. I realized that the men never talked to each other like that, at least not in English. Then his eyes suddenly warmed up. I could feel it. He smiled sheepishly, then said: "Why, you glad?"

I told him I was just bored.

"*Bored.* What means *bored*?"

I tried to pull in as much German as I could. When you've knocked around a lot, you pick up languages the way some people pick up men. Out of nowhere, a suitable word came to me. *Langweilig.* Boring. The word just hit him. I told him the work was *sehr, sehr langweilig.* He smiled. His biceps flexed, and he started rubbing his stomach, so that shots of hairy belly and chest came through. As cold as it was up on deck, it was hot down in the hold. But whatever the cause, *langweilig* started Hans rattling away in German about a mile-a-minute, and much faster than I could understand. But I did catch that he, too, was bored. I caught on to that. Bored, and lonely. I'm not sure what the word for lonely was, but I knew it was there. I could see it, even in the dark, on his face.

I liked seeing that he was lonely. I'd even forgotten how lonely I got on a ship, even with Casey around to pop in and josh with me every now and then. I got up from the floor, where I'd been pretending to check out more of the stock numbers, and where I'd really been checking out Hans' crotch. I'd gotten a great view. I saw the part where his heavy balls had been making impressions in his dirty, white seaman's pants. I was sure he didn't wear underwear, but I couldn't see the outline of the head of his dick, either.

As soon as I was up, clipboard in hand; he got closer to me. Very very close. I realized how dark it was. I'd gotten accustomed to the dim light down in the hold, but now with him just about a nose away from me, it seemed even darker. I could feel his warm breath on my face. What was going to happen now? I remained really still. His shoulders shifted; both his big hands went up to my shoulders. Then I felt his right hand gently touch the left side of my neck. My mouth went dry. "Beer?" he asked. "I go up, get beer, be back!"

Now, things were definitely looking better. I watched him climb the stairs up at the other end of the hold, several rows of barrels away. Just before the hatch door closed, he rang out to me, "Be-back-right-away!" The hatch door clicked shut, and I was in darkness again. I loved the sound of it: "Be-back-right-away." That was merchant marine talk. Everything was "be-back-right-away!" I'd met Nigerian sailors who knew eight words of English: Coca-Cola, beer, pussy, money, and "Be-back-right-away!"

I scribbled down some more of the numbers, and decided that I'd over-booked the job. It would not take me as long as I thought. I could have the whole fucking job finished in a little more than two hours; then I could grab some sleep and get up early in the morning to type out some shit to give to the Old Man. The Captain would have to go through the manifest, but he actually didn't knew crap about what went on down in the holds. And this was one time I was very happy for that.

I'd already gone through about four hundred barrels of turps, oils, greas-es, and I was now at something called naval jelly, which is not something you stick on your belly button. Naval jelly is a very thick form of grease. It looks like a viscous, high grade of cum—maybe darker. It's used as a water proofer and as a soluble for other greases. In other words, you always use one greasy product to dissolve another one. I thought about that for a moment. Perhaps it should be a law of life itself. I liked the smell of naval stores. The stuff smelled strong, piney, with just a tang of salt in it. It reminded me of boats and men.

A moment later, Hans came back down from the mess locker with half a dozen large, cold bottles of dark German beer. Real lager. I wondered what he was going to use to open them, but he knew exactly how to pry off the caps with the metal rims of the naval barrels. "Here," he said, softly, like this was a great secret between us, and he offered me the first bottle he opened. I lifted the bottle to drink. It was thick, delicious, and cold. The head of the beer rose, creamed, and foamed on my lips. It swirled in my mouth. I swallowed some and then licked the sweet saltiness off my lips, while I watched Hans. He heaved his head back and chugged half the bot-tle. I was *sehr* impressed. "*Gut?*" he asked. I told him it sure was. We soon finished the first two bottles, then he opened two more.

I took my time drinking the second beer, but he was rapidly into his third. I knew the Germans could drink beer, but Hans was a professional. I smiled. It got warmer down in the hold, especially with another body next to me. Suddenly, after I was through with the second bottle, the beer hit me.

37

Technically, I was supposed to be working. By regulations, I wasn't supposed to unbutton my collar and take off my tie. But I said fuck it and I did.

"You hot?" Hans asked me. I told him I was. He smiled and immediately stripped off his white tee shirt. He was just a seaman, so that was all, by regs, he had to wear. I, being an asshole petty officer—hardly above an office boy—had to put up with the tie-and-clean-white-shirt routine. I still ate with the men, but I was supposed to be a notch or so above them. I looked up at him. A quick flavor from his armpits hit me. It wasn't rank, just piquant. Salt. Sweat. Nice. Hans was bigger than I remembered, even from that shower we took together. Now, I couldn't get my eyes off him. He had beautiful, hard looking nipples, that begged me to want to play with them. But right then, being slightly tipsy, all I could do was smile.

I must have looked like a Cheshire cat.

"Why you smiling?" he asked. "Want another beer?"

I wasn't sure what to tell him. I was smiling because I sincerely wanted his cock in my mouth, but all I could say was that if I drank another beer, I'd have to piss my brains out. "Piss brains out!" he repeated, and then laughed some more. Then he started to rub some of the heat away from his chest and push at his nipples. One of them, I could see, was harder than the other. His head nodded at me. "You want to *pees* brains out?"

Then it dawned on me how funny that sounded.

"No, Hans, I want to piss piss."

He laughed again. "I got to piss, too." His hand ran down to his crotch, which now poked well out of his baggy whites. Now I could definitely see some of his thick dick in there.

I nodded my head, and walked with him, weaving back and forth both from the beer and some of the movement of the boat, halfway down the length of the hold. I'm sure he could see I was tipsy. Sometimes I had to hold on to the barrels. Then I grabbed at him. We stopped moving, and he laughed while I held on to him, right under his bare armpits. He looked at me, and I could feel his breathing in my face. I could taste the German beer in the air from him. I wanted to eat it right out of his mouth, but didn't. I pretended to tickle him, but ended up pulling at his nipples. Like it was a game. He smiled innocently, as I did it. I think he was only pretending that he didn't notice, because he never moved away.

Halfway down the length of the hold, there was a place reserved for guys working down there to piss. It was supposed to be a single toilet, but actually it was just a drain used for emptying mop buckets. The drain was slightly sunk into the floor. It was about a half foot in diameter. We all knew you could piss there; each hold had one. "This best piss place," Hans joked. He laughed some more, and then unbuttoned his pants.

I asked him what was so funny. He started howling. Spitting from laughter. Then he calmed down, and said, "Can not speak in English this."

"Why not?" I looked directly at him.

He suddenly turned from me, embarrassed. He nodded his head. "Alright. Piss hard-on, you call it?"

I told him that was the word, and then, quickly—I admit it was crazy, but I wasn't going to wait long enough to talk myself out of this situation—I reached into his fly and started to fish around for his pecker. I found it soon. It was wonderful. Large, fat around, I swear, as my wrist, and, like most Germans, uncut. I pulled the head out of his pants, and he didn't fight me at all. He just stood there, and then took the rest of his cock out himself, and held it, at the base, down there next to his swelling balls.

"This is good," he said, in a low, very German voice, half sex and half growl. "I like my *Schwantz*. You like it, too?" He was hard as a rock, and his dick started to glow with heat. I must say, I couldn't help myself after that. It was too much not to get into. So I started to suck him off. I pushed the head of his meat, with the foreskin rolled back, into my mouth. The head tasted great. Very clean, with just a certain warm, crotch smell to it. I pushed my nose down to his balls for a second, and got a light whiff of them, too. They smelled great. I wondered if he'd just washed his privates off. The smell of shower soap was still on them, although I don't think I would have minded the slightest hint of cheese.

"This is my sex stick," he said. "You like it?"

I stopped sucking him long enough to tell him—I loved it. Then I went back down on him. I forgot about pissing myself, since my boner was now pretty much as big as a house. (Okay—truth—a small house.)

Suddenly, he said to me, "Smoky, you want me to play, too?" I wasn't sure what he meant, till he pulled me up and with one arm held me against a row of barrels, and then with his left hand started to unzip my pants. "Let me see what you got," he smiled.

I got my dick out, and he caressed it with his large hands, working it bigger and harder with both of them. The scene was getting too hot for pants, so I managed to get out of my trousers, while Hans pulled his baggy whites off.

Hans was then totally bare-assed, but would you believe I still had my shirt and tie on? They were somewhat loosened. They looked like they'd been put through a wringer, but I still had them on. That started to turn me on even more—that I was still half-dressed while Hans bent down over me, and put his thick mouth on my meat. We started to trade head for a while, and he sucked me while I fed him my dick, then we reversed. I'm not sure why I didn't just get down on the floor with him, but I didn't. I don't know how I managed to keep my head and not turn into a rutting pig, crawling around on the hard, dirty floor of the hold, while I ate Hans' cock, but I'm

39

proud to say I didn't. A man's gotta have some pride, right?

I'm also not sure if Hans normally sucked cock. Maybe he just got so hot down in the hold—from the beer and the moment—that he'd do anything. Believe me, that happened fairly often on boats, if you were lucky enough to be in the right place at the right time.

After we'd been doing this for a while (but to tell you the truth, I had no idea how long), I realized that neither of us could come because of all the beer we'd drunk. There was too much liquid in us. Hans must have had the same idea. "I better piss," he said.

I let him go for a minute. He aimed himself right over the drain. Now everything got silent down in the hold. I could tell he was holding his breath and waiting for his dick to soften to get the pee out. Then, through the darkness down there over the drain, I saw a thick, golden, warm spray. He exhaled, so that his whole body relaxed.

I was tempted. Drunk. I knew it. But I didn't know what to do. I couldn't figure it out in this inebriated state: if I got any piss on me, I was afraid it was going to dribble some of it all over on my pants—and I knew I'd have to put them back on to go back up. But I'd gone so far, and I was so turned on by everything, including the outrageous danger of the situation, that I said, why not? I grabbed his soft cock while he was peeing and he squirted right on my crotch. It felt great on my legs—warm, heavier than water. Some of it ran down my balls. Hans started laughing again, but he shut up quickly when I started drinking his piss directly from his cock. The feeling of his thick, meaty dick head and the warm piss running down my throat was great. His piss came in blasts and between the blasts his cock would soften a bit. Then he'd blast again, and get hard again.

I took a lot of it, and a lot of it drizzled over my legs and lower body. I decided to take off my shirt. I did this while he finished pissing. A few drops of the yellow liquid shone at the end of his peter, until the head started to retreat back into his thick, German foreskin.

I pulled his foreskin back and played with his meat some more. The skin of his foreskin felt slightly loose over his large, firm pecker.

"Now me," he said and laughed, and I obliged him by peeing on him. He loved it, and I liked watching it. Piss splashed against his heavy legs and big thighs, swirling with coarse, blondish hair. Suddenly, I wanted to lick out his navel. It was thick, and ridged up slightly over his belly muscles. I ran my tongue into, and then worked my mouth down to his cock. He grabbed at his large, full balls, and became more excited—became really out of it, like he was in that hot, grunting, animal state that great sex is all about, whether we want to admit it or not. Then—I don't know why, I wasn't sucking him that hard—he started to come. I can still taste the fresh, clean flavor of his jism, mixed with the yellow, saltiness of some piss that remained on him.

While he came, I jacked myself off, just gobbling up as much of his swollen dick as I could in my mouth.

We kicked back for a while, as reality set back in. You know, the hold of the ship. Dark. Are we going to get out of this alive and not get noticed? That sort of stuff. I jumped up and sat on a barrel. It felt nice and cold next to my extremely warm ass.

"That was *sehr gut*," Hans said. "That is why I came down here."

"You did?" I asked, surprised. It was really dark down in the hold now. I knew it'd be black as hell up on decks. I could feel the ship moving under me. It's a great feeling, once you're used to it. "What made you think I'd be sex?"

"I been watching you," he said and smiled. I kissed him on his large mouth, and then ran my tongue over his eyelids. He'd been watching me? Now that was a switch. The whole time I thought I'd been watching him. Then I remembered those small, intense blue eyes. They did work you over, like a soft tongue.

I felt a bit groggy, from the heat, the dark, and the great sex. With a little bit of luck, we could get our clothes back on, and dash for the showers next to my cabin. After that, Hans would have to get back to his shift. But first we'd have to climb out of the hold, and hope that nobody—especially anyone with a nose for piss, beer, and cum—was around.

Luckily, no one was up on that part of the lower deck where the hatch was. I did see the Old Man striding around at the far end of the deck, trying hard to look interested and busy. I think that was what most captains did in public. He didn't see me. He might have been just a tad tipsy himself—I knew the Old Man went in for a usual martini or two after the sun went down. We got out of the hatch quickly, and I whispered for Hans to meet me in the shower.

Well, he did. We stayed in the shower for about twenty minutes. Since the shower was fairly private—I shared it with another petty officer whom I knew was asleep before his shift, I got to soap Hans down the way I wanted to. Slowly. Nicely. With much attention to his feet, ass, and balls. His ass was large and muscular—not one of those tiny, twinkie asses that so many guys go for—but it really turned me on. So much so that I didn't even hear Casey come by the head, and I thought I was going to have a minor heart attack when he popped in, fully dressed, to have a look around. He caught me on my knees, starting to go again at Han's dick.

I sprang to my feet.

He only smiled, and pretended to be shocked. "Busy house tonight, boys?" he asked, and shook his head.

I told him to shut up and get lost, and turned the shower head right into

41

his direction. One second more, and I would have drenched him. He left the can, and I managed to get Hans back to my cabin and into my bed before he was due on decks.

"He a friend yours?" Hans asked.

"You could say that," I said.

"I think so," Hans said. "You call him your *buddy*?"

"No, just a friend."

"*Gut*. Maybe I be your buddy now."

I managed to smile at that. It seemed like this was going to be a great trip. A few minutes later, Hans left my cabin, and I decided to grab some sleep before finishing that manifest that the Old Man wanted. I shut my eyes, and drifted off for a few minutes, but woke up again, horny as ever. I knew then that all I could think about was getting my hands back on Hans.

TASTE

I used to like to suck him off in the middle of the night. I wasn't sure if he was sleeping or not. Sometimes he must have been pretending. This excited me—the mystery of it: that maybe he wasn't sleeping; but maybe he actually was. I would find his large, swollen cock in the darkness, and it would rise up in the warmth inside of my mouth. Larger. Not really throbbing, but just larger. I would taste him—a slight tang of urine, maybe; then the thicker, wilder stuff that excited me just before he came. It was as if he was floating in a bed of dreams and sex itself, and I was guiding him, touching him every place, feeling his warm, firm chest—no hair to speak of, but great meaty tits that thickened when he got excited or I excited him—and I would push him along on this coast of wild, half-dreaming sex, until he gushed right into my mouth, the head of his cock expanding, fanning out in a delta of thickened, hot flesh.

Now, I ask you: who in the hell wouldn't want that? I know this may be a strange story to you. That is, some people might find it a little funny, some a little strange. But it is really about one of the great cementing experiences between humans. And by this, I am *not* referring to a shared sense of taste. I'm talking about plain old, decent, hard-working sex.

43

Okay: begin. I picked him up at the baths, two weeks earlier. Or maybe it was that Jim had picked me out. We were in the orgy room, and he suddenly appeared out of the darkness and grabbed my dick. He was bigger than me. I'm fairly slender: hairy chest, curly hair, blue eyes. Actually, we were almost the same height, but he was stockier. He had delicious brawny shoulders, and the kind of deep, silken chest that guys like me have wet dreams about.

"Come on with me," he said. I didn't answer him, but just followed. We went back to his room. "I just got in from Seattle," he informed me in his small cubicle of a room. He looked straight at me. "You're the best, first thing I've seen here tonight."

I laughed. Seattle? Alright. That made sense. I must have spelled NEW YORK all over the place—darker, slightly Mediterranean type. Read Jewish/Italian/Greco-Spanish. Take your pick. I didn't think guys like me were all over Seattle. But then I'd never been to Seattle. This did not stop us from getting into it from every which-away. He had an insatiable ass, mouth, and dick. I must say, he was as much of a sexaholic as I was, and I gave it my darnedest to satisfy him—and myself—as best I could. We former Boy Scouts know how to "help other people at all times," let me tell you. Whoever said that sex with a stranger was the devil's playground knew this devil very well, and Jim York, from Seattle, Washington, certainly stuck the devil right into me—as well as his fat, yummy dick and his mouth—which he used like a trumpet player, triple-noting on the underside of my pecker.

Okay, perhaps I did break the first rule. I ended up sleeping with him. *Strange.* Here *he* was in New York (as he told me) on business, for under two weeks, and he checks into the baths, then settles on the first guy who takes his fancy in the orgy room, and then he stays with him (*me*) for the whole night.

It was the kind of thing you either had to be very dumb to do, or very smart. And I have to admit, from the vantage point of several years later, that I wasn't smart enough at that time to know the difference.

"Hey, you know what the chances are of this happening?" he asked me at seven in the morning. It was Sunday. I knew there were still herds of men out there all over New York, on the pre-church shift, actively praying for sex. And we were in the cathedral itself. I had no idea what he was talking about. My mouth felt cottony, my balls felt numb, my ass felt—wonderful— and I was ready to go at him again.

"Tell me," I said.

He nodded his head slowly. "Alright. The chances of me finding some one like you at the baths on a Saturday night in New York come out to," he paused for just a second: "One-hundred-and-twenty thousand to one."

My eyes closed. There was a lot of sleep left in them, sleep I did not get that night. But my curiosity was piqued. I asked him how he figured out these odds.

He got up, naked, so I could see his wonderful, hard, man-sexy butt, and opened a small clothes locker. He dragged out a pocket calculator. "I figure 200 guys come here at one time. Right? They change every three hours. That's six hundred a night. Saturday night, you know? Full capacity. Everything's going full tilt. Now, there are eight baths in New York. So, for the argument, say that each one of them could contain ..."

He had it worked out. He was right. The odds were one-hundred-and twenty thousand to one. Not that he'd just trick with some one, but find some one who fitted exactly what he wanted, sex-wise, temperament, etc. I decided there was nothing I could do about this at this time, except suck his dick again, until we decided something else to do.

So, we did this—and that, a lot of *that*, believe me, a lot of that: heavy mouth kissing, touching, rubbing, sucking, *etc.*—then took a shower. Then we went back to his room, and then I wasn't sure what to do next. I knew we'd reached those limits of sexual intimacy that intimate strangers reach fairly quickly, at least we'd reached them for the moment—and the cold, cruel world outside—the one that said, "I don't know you, and you really don't know me," was quickly setting in.

"What are you doing this evening?" he asked. He had a kind of simple, wonderfully silly smile on his face.

I hesitated. I wasn't really sure. How far could I take this? Should I ask him up to my place, or should we meet in a bar? I felt funny about pursuing this. Suppose I decided that I actually *didn't* like him that much? Now, a bar might be the cooler thing to do—it was always easier to get rid of somebody in a bar. You could always do a 'Hey, there's my cousin Tillie from Idaho' routine, and get lost ...

"Why don't we have dinner?" he asked, butting right into my indecision. "Have you ever been to the Cattle Baron?"

I shut my eyes. I started to giggle a bit. The Cattle Baron was a huge, strictly-for-tourists-and/or-visiting-salesmen-on-expense-account place in mid-town Manhattan. Steaks. Over-sized shrimp cocktails. French fries made from half a baking potato. Waitresses in Miss Kitty drag. This was not the sort of place smart New Yorkers went to for a good time. "No," I answered. He suggested we go there. He could put the whole thing on his expense account.

I got home to my small dump in the West Fifties, flopped into bed, got about three more hours' sleep, and had some coffee. Now I was starting to feel more like myself. My *authentic* self. My *real* self, aside from the self that you became at the baths or in a bar. I'm not sure what self I was there, but it

45

certainly wasn't the self I was at home. I put on a new Vivaldi album I'd just bought, read the *Times*, called two friends who told me what a dreadful Saturday night they'd had, and who asked me, separately, what I was doing for dinner. When I told them the Cattle Baron, they both almost dropped the phone. Then came the laughter. "It's a joke, right?" the first one said. By the second phone call, I had the explanation down pat. "No, not a joke," I said. "I met him last night. The baths. He's from Seattle. I guess you could say he's a real guy."

My first friend, Jack, another writer, tried to talk sense to me. "Listen, Smokes—you are not into *real* people—you're a writer. If you were into real people, you'd give up your life and start making *real* money. That's what *real* people do."

"'Se-cuse me," I said.

Jack started chuckling again. My second friend, Vance, my Neo-Abstract-Expressionist-and-Performance-Art young friend from the East Village, this scrumptious, thin, young man with the vanilla-ice-cream body and the sausage cock, was more serious. "The Cattle Baron? Hmmm," he replied. "Smoky, just think of it like it's all one BIG piece of art."

Dorothy, our waitress, led us back into the Buffalo Bill Room. Jim had arrived wearing a coat and tie to my place. I decided to wear corduroy slacks and a decent, white shirt, tieless. We took a cab over. Dorothy gave Jim a knowing look. "I know you gentlemen must have a lot to talk over, so we're gonna give you a quiet corner," she said. She left. "She thinks you're a score," Jim said to me.

"A *what*?"

"Somebody I'm going to sell something to. Pitch? Get it?" Dorothy came back with a tray of hors d'oeuvres big as an elephant's feed trough. In most New York restaurants, hors d'oeuvres look like nose pickings. Not here. This was big. Cheese, bread, celery, shrimp: the whole deal. It was enough for any normal New Yorker to make a full meal from. I looked around the room. The other diners looked like they came from a foreign species. Fat, business types. "The idea of this place," Jim explained, "is that you eat until you bust. The company's paying for it." Jim went about ordering two large steaks. "Rare," he said, "but no blood." Dorothy and her serving colleague, Annie, much boobs poking out of her waist cincher, brought them back on huge, hot, pewter platters. The steaks were large enough to send you into protein overdose—or vegetarianism. "Hope you guys enjoy!" Annie said, and winked.

I have to admit the steak was good. Crunchy, peppery, but no blood. I could only eat about half of it, and two Scotches, one rusty nail, a lot of red wine, and an after-dinner drink that was very sweet and smelled somewhat like lighter fluid. Boy, was I lit. Jim was starting to look abso-fucking-lutely wonderful. Slightly wobbly; glowing. They were right: candy was dandy, but liquor was definitely quicker.

I decided I'd better go to the men's room, or else pass out on the table. I got up, while Jim smiled at me, and I excused myself. The Buffalo Bill Room suddenly looked very huge and very dark at the same time. And everybody, for the first time, looked *very* friendly. They didn't seem to mind the fact at all that I was grabbing the backs of their chairs just to stand up *and* walk.

This type of life can kill you, I decided, but somehow I found the men's room, which was located around several very tight corners—not kind at all to drunk people—in the basement. It, too, was large and dark. Then I realized that when you've had three times more alcohol than your nature intends, everything starts to spread out and become rather difficult to get to. The bathroom attendant, an older black man, must have been used to this, and kindly pointed me into the direction of the large, marble sinks that came equipped with ornate gilt knobs and fixtures. I knew I had to get some cold water on my face, but I couldn't figure out how these things that looked like flying dolphins and water nymphs worked. He turned on the cold water for me, and then offered me a towel, some yucky pink cologne, the use of a comb, and a bottle of red mouthwash. He smiled at me knowingly. "Lissen," I droned, "I'm not gonna take up residence here ... I jus' needed some of that cold water on my face."

A few seconds later, Jim appeared. He asked me if I was alright. I beamed. Boy, it was nice to see a familiar face. Didn't I know him? His face was starting to look like a marshmallow, but it was okay. Jesus, I liked this guy. Maybe I was falling for him. I hiccupped. Maybe I was just falling all over him. The attendant starting hovering over both of us—I was back at the sink, still spraying water on my face and trying to stand up on both feet—when Jim offered him a couple of dollars to go out and get him a cigar. "Good panatela," Jim specified. Wow, I thought, the guy even knows Italian. The attendant left. Jim found the lock to the men's room, snapped it shut, and took my cock out. He started gently squeezing it in his hand, and I started to like it. Even the Cattle Baron was getting to be great fun. I asked him what he was going to do when the guy came back. "Don't worry. They've been through worse before. Salesmen are notorious, you know."

He went down and started sucking my dick, just for a second. This was very nice. A moment later, there was a knock on the door. I managed to zip up again, and the attendant, with three customers waiting, flopped in. Jim had his arm around me. "My friend's not feeling too well," he explained to everybody. They all smiled knowingly, like we were in the middle of some *rite de passage.* Then Jim took his cigar, and we walked out.

47

We got back to the table, and found the bill waiting. Jim sat down, took out his plastic, and suddenly two rather professional looking ladies whom we noticed hanging around the bar, trumped up. "Looking for company?" one asked.

Jim smiled, said no, and handed the other, who looked like she'd seen many better days, a five. "Buy yourself a drink," he advised, and we left.

The air felt great outside. It was still early, and a purple haze of neon and late dusk wrapped itself around mid-town Manhattan. It was not yet summer, but it would be soon. Sinus season, I called it—that evil transition into warmer weather. It closed up my nose, but opened up every other sense. I suggested that despite my disgraceful state of inebriation (which I was starting to get an excellent kick out of), we walk back to my place. It was hard for me to control myself, and at one point we ducked into an empty alcove, and I groped the good hell out of Jim. He looked at me like he just couldn't believe what was going on—there, close to Times Square. I just laughed.

On the way back, Jim kept stopping at glass-walled, tourist art galleries, the ones that sold paintings of smiling Amish families, and snow geese, or sad-eyed kids and clowns. I laughed at all the junk on the walls, until I realized that Jim was *serious*, and despite my being exceedingly hot for him and wanting to get him back between the sheets as quickly as possible, he was actually eyeing this stuff to buy it. He kept insisting that one ghastly piece after the next—a Spanish dancer with a velvet rose stuck in her mouth, a seascape with bits of real balsa wood glued to it—would look great in his collection. "I collect," he said, seriously.

After the fourth gallery, we finally made it back. We had our clothes off in a jiffy, and half an hour later, I passed right out with his wonderful dick straight up my ass.

He moved in two nights later. It was one of those situations that you drift into without thinking hard about it. He was scheduled to stay in New York for nine more days, and it seemed silly for him to spend so much money at a hotel, when he could be using the same money to have fun with me. It has been said that sex can not keep two people together; but if you want it bad enough, it can't keep you apart either. Jim had a great number of things to do during the days—lots of scores to talk to—but at night we did very regular kinds of things: ate out at showy restaurants that he'd heard about back home. Went to buddy movies where one buddy was always chasing around with the other buddy, but they didn't sleep together. Saw several bad plays that salesmen feel they aren't supposed to leave New York without seeing. I introduced him to a great number of my friends. He would at some point in the conversation bring out his pocket calculator and explain to them the odds on the weather, the Russians actually taking Manhattan ("If they could land by sea, about 758 to one."), and the Mets winning this thing called the Pennant. He also had this strange way of referring to my friends as "Sir." Since they'd never had this done before, except in a sexual situation, they kept taking me aside one by one and telling me how lucky I was.

"One-hundred-and-sixty-five thousand to one," Jim said to me flatly. That was the odds on his staying nine days and things working out. Since we'd started out as strangers, except in that strangest and most wonderful of areas, sex, I was starting to see that they were pretty steep, but honest odds. I was also starting to feel that this odds business showed some truthfulness: although the sex thing with Jim York was not turning stale as fast as I thought, everything else was starting to gather dust and curl up around the edges pretty damn fast. The truth was: I was terribly bored with him. He came from a different world: the so-called real one, out there in America itself—and I was working too hard at being New York, for whatever that was worth. I tried to think about the reverse of the situation, and decided that I might end up boring him just as badly if I ever went back with him to the suburbs of Seattle, where he had a two-bedroom apartment. One bedroom "filled with art and my books," he explained. "I've read everything Stephen King's ever written," he added, then asked: "You ever heard of him?"

I felt that I had made in-roads, though. I felt proud that I'd given him a little polish, a little big-city sophistication. I got him to stop using the brand of reeked-to-hell cologne he doused himself with. It was called "Conquistador," and by the time he stopped, the scent of it—like cinnamon chewing gum and gardenias—had spread like the ravages of jungle ants through my apartment. Even the toilet paper in my bathroom stunk of it. I decided to give him a bottle of *Citron Imperiale*, a light, lemony decoction that carried a pedigree back to Napoleon and that cost bucks. He loved the simple, imitation cut-crystal bottle and the grosgrain ribbon tastefully wrapped around the ground-glass stopper. It produced a wonderful beam on his clear, blond face. "You bought this for *me*?" he asked.

I told him I did. We stripped and went to bed. I wrapped my arms and tongue around his chest, and bit into his tits and neck like a wild dog. He was still punching the right buttons for me in the bedroom, if only I could manage to keep him there indefinitely. I guessed it all came down to a question of taste. I wondered why taste was such a big deal, anyway. I wanted to taste him alright, and I couldn't wait to get my mouth on his fat balls again. But those damn pictures of the cheery Amish families, the balsa wood seascapes, and the knit, polyester shirts he bought by the case ("Cheaper that way; you get 30% off the discount price. Let me tell you how much money I save.") were driving me kind of nuts.

Well, at least I got rid of the Conquistador cologne. That was a victory. Small, but it made me proud. I saw him take it into the bathroom and flush it down the john. In a way, I was almost sorry Jim did that. Perhaps I should have kept it to kill cockroaches with.

It was the last night that he was going to be with me in New York that things got rotten. I was set to go with him to the airport the next day. In a limousine, yet. "The company won't mind," he told me. "You'll love it. They have a real bar in back."

We went out to Mama Louisa's, a touristy Italian restaurant he'd always heard about. I'm not sure why, but Jim always picked those places where we would be taken for two out-of-town salesmen. The hostess, this very fat lady in very thin, very high heels asked, "Are you two with the National Light Bulb Show?" Jim smiled and told her he wasn't in light bulbs. "Computer relays."

She nodded her head which had a huge amount of hair piled on it. "Yeh," she said. "Computers are important these days." She led us to a small table in the back, and then a troop of waiters brought out what seemed like half a ton of freshly defrosted Italian dishes and whole loaves of garlic bread. There were strolling mandolin players. We polished off two bottles of Chianti. I started to forget about almost everything, except the possibility of throwing up so much pasta.

I groaned when we finally got up from the table. Luckily, we could walk back to my place again. I needed the walk and the air. "You know, I like you," he said on the way back. It was really touching. I had to hold myself back from wanting to jump him on the street, and peel his clothes off right there. But we did get home and I started to strip off his shirt—another of his famous polyester knits.

"Wait a second," he ordered. I did. "Close your eyes." I did that, too. I was hoping he'd produce a pair of handcuffs or run some marvelous dildo up my ass, but instead he took out from the living room closet this large thing wrapped in brown paper. "Oh," I said.

"I decided you had to have it," was all he said. I carefully unwrapped it, hoping it wasn't the worst. It was. It was the most awful painting I'd ever seen in my life. Something called "African Veldt"—a herd of zebras done on black linen in day-glow colors, with real pieces of "Authentic Jungle Grass" glued to the background.

I didn't know what to say. I kept trying to smile, and then suddenly—without even controlling what was coming out, I said, "I can't accept this. I feel like it's—"

He understood immediately. His face fell. I felt like a shit and a half. He walked into the bathroom, which I knew—absolutely knew—still smelled deeply of Conquistador. He came out with the bottle of *Citron Imperiale* I'd given him and handed it back to me. "I think I'm going to leave," he said. He went to get his bags. "I can stay in a hotel."

I tried to hold him back, and told him that I was sure "African Veldt" cost a lot more than he could afford, which was a lie, but one that we call a socially excusable one.

"That's not the point," Jim said. "I just wanted you to have it."

So I took it and pretended to be extremely happy with it, and decided, while we were in bed that night, that as soon as Jim left, "African Veldt" was going back into the living room closet (in the same brown wrapper it arrived in), and I was going to have a very good time with Jim that night. And I did.

We woke up fairly late the next morning, after doing an almost unbearable amount of sexual activity, the type that would send the D.A.R. and the Salvation Army into near-fatal shock, and maybe even some envy. Some men seem to have everything—at least sexually, physically—that you want, and Jim was one of them. If I could pick men off of trees and bring them home, put them into the refrigerator, and just eat them when I wanted—before they started to go all mushy and I started to tire of the taste—well, certainly Jim York would be one of them. But the thought of two weeks in Seattle with him, like he'd been seriously suggesting, just did not "compute" as they would say in his business.

We took a shower and carried on like hot, naked seals in the water—I had my tongue up his ass so long I thought I might drown—then we dressed and I had some coffee. The limo came at three, and we went out to JFK, getting slightly sloshed along the way. He told me that business-wise, he'd done very well in New York, and everything-else-wise—he just beamed.

We got out of the limo, and I shook his hand, very business-like, and then got back in, and the driver took me home. A few days later, I got a very nice card from him, and "African Veldt" was still up on my living room wall. My friends came back and discussed it intelligently. Vance thought it was a piece of "Post-Modern sensibility that shows a critically earnest technique, though a bit mannered." I closed my eyes for a moment and tried not to look at "African Veldt" while I looked at Vance; then we got our clothes off as quickly as possible. With Vance lying under me, I forgot all about "African Veldt," or any veldt for that matter. Jack, my writer friend, thought it was a "stone gas" and "one of the ugliest things I've ever seen in all my life," but he made me promise to give it to him if I ever got tired of it myself.

Strangely enough, though, I did not. And, about eight months later, I flew to Seattle to see Jim York. He picked me up in a large, gas-guzzling car, and then I went back to his suburban Seattle apartment and I quickly got used to his bad art and his taste in books.

As for his taste, he was yummy. He cooked well, and we had great sex, sometimes more of it than even I could stand. One night, after he'd fucked me so long and so well—with smooth, tender, hard, fabulous strokes; know what I mean?—I sat up in bed, looking at the ceiling, while he slept. Then I remembered something my mother told me after I came out to her and she realized I wasn't going to be bringing girls home, but boys. "Listen," she said seriously. "No matter what a man looks like, ask him these three questions: Can he fix a flat tire? Can he fix a leaky faucet? And, can he fix a running toilet."

Her very wise advice kept running through my own mind. Then I fell asleep next to Jim.

THE PLATINUM RING

I met Dev at the Yukon, a bar in the East Seventies. Despite its name, the Yukon was as far away from the Wild West—and from leather or Western/Levi bars—as you could get. In fact, it was one of those places that swankier guys from a generation older than my own—I'm thirty-six—would have called "cuff-linky." Crisp, white shirts. Dark suits. Ties. Very dry martinis. It was an after-work crowd. I just happened to be in the neighborhood about six o' clock one evening. I'd been helping a friend who lived nearby edit a piece for his college alumni magazine called "How To Make It In New York Five Years After Graduation"; believe me, one topic I knew *very* little about. Walking back to catch the bus—it was a cold evening in November—I saw the place and decided to try for some warm company.

Dev was alone in a corner, drinking a dry martini by himself. He was compact, medium build, with a good face—regular, nice features, great white teeth and a wild smile that I noticed quickly. The Yukon was not really a place to smile in. It was a kind of business bar, whose main business was discrete men with money picking up tricks, usually equally discrete, younger men with less money. It was a good place to get married, in a gay way, for a while. I never really made out well there. I was certainly not marrying for money material. I didn't have enough to splurge on meals in East

53

Side restaurants, and I was way past, both chronologically and psychologically, the twinkie age. In other words, I didn't look like the kind of guy older men rush up to buy drinks for.

So I was surprised when Dev approached me. "What are you drinking?" he asked. I told him a beer, and he called one of their twinkies-in-ties over and ordered me a Canadian lager. I felt embarrassed, since I didn't have enough money for the next round, especially dry martinis.

"What are you doing here?" he asked me. His smile, with sharp dimples on either side, revealing perfect teeth, kind of exploded, like he was going to break out at any second into uncontrollable laughter. That smile, so explosive, so uncontrolled, seemed strange in a guy wearing a dark, banker's pin stripe suit; black, Brooks Brothers tassel loafers; and a gold-green-and-maroon-silk "Old School" tie. Then I saw that it was a nervous, making-up-for-shyness smile, and I warmed up to him and realized we were close to the same age, give or take a couple of years.

"I was just in the neighborhood," I explained to him, and thanked him for the beer. Then, suddenly, I felt very tongue-tied around him. Quickly it occurred to me that he *really* belonged in this swank-ass bar, and I didn't. And I *knew* I didn't. More executive types started coming in and they smiled at Devlin—as he introduced himself to me—and then he quickly introduced me to about ten of his bar friends. I hated that. I tried not to be sullen, but I was not interested in them, and I knew they'd quickly forget me, so why should I know their names?

He finished his martini, and I started to panic. It must have registered on my face. He asked me if I wanted another beer, and I told him that I really had to leave. I knew that at any moment his friends were going to start making plans for dinner at little foreign restaurants with big American prices, and I wasn't in the mood to be that chummy with this group on a Tuesday night.

"Leave?" His eyes shot at me, and he smiled again, but this time with more twinkle than shyness. "That's a good idea, let's leave." He grabbed my arm and took me over to the coat check and took out his top coat, a light-colored, camel cashmere number with large pockets; the type of coat you don't put anything in the pockets, except maybe a couple of theatre tickets. He noticed that I was only wearing a Levi jacket over my sweater, which was *not* cashmere, but a khaki field sweater I'd pulled out of an Army-Navy store in Brooklyn. "Nothing checked?" he asked considerately. I shook my head no.

It was very black outside, but the air was fresh after the Yukon. I'd forgotten how obnoxious being in places crammed with cologned-up bodies can be. He called a cab, and one stopped immediately at the sight of his elegant coat. I was impressed. We piled into the back—him first; he told the cabby his address, which was on East Fiftieth Street, then he settled into the corner, just behind the driver, and pulled me over to him. "Nervous?" he whispered. I told him I was. Just a bit; also excited. I didn't expect things to go this far, this fast. I reached under his camel coat and started to feel him up. He smiled again, and then suddenly—in the cab and all—started to kiss me very hard.

We got out of the cab, and he overtipped the driver, who acted properly impressed. Then I realized where we were. It was that little alley that runs parallel to the East River, called Beekman Place. His doorman let us in, smiled at Mr. Hanson, and completely ignored me. The elevator boy did the same thing. We got out into a very narrow hallway with only two apartments on the floor. He unlocked his door.

"Careful, don't trip," he warned me, then snapped on a wall lamp. The living room, sunken three steps below the entranceway, went on for days, at least forty feet. It ended up with a wonderful view of the East River. I told him how beautiful his apartment was. We sat down together on a large, blue couch, upholstered in a Chinese silk, peony design. "Do you want something to eat or drink?" he asked me.

"I think I want something to eat," I said softly and started to unbutton his shirt. Something told me that if this wasn't going to last forever, I should at least enjoy every moment of it while I could. He smiled that great, open-mouthed smile of his, and I realized now that his eyes were deep green, like jade, and I was getting very hot, and it wasn't from the central heating.

I unknotted his tie, and finished his shirt, while I managed to take off my clothes at the same time. This wasn't easy. "I thought you were shy," he said to me. I told him I was. "That's good," he said. "I don't like pushy men, the kind who feel they can buy their way through the world."

He took me into his bedroom while we still had our pants and shoes on. I'd left a trail of clothes through the living room, the adjacent dining room, and the hall to the bedroom. He asked me if I wanted to take a shower first, and I told him we'd take a shower after.

The bedroom was almost completely dark. It had another view of the river. He stripped back the goose down comforter, and then started to untie my black, Army-Navy watch boots. While he did this, I started to kiss his chest, running my lips down it, licking at the light, ash-blond fur on it that swirled around his hard little nipples in snowflake patterns. I took one of his tits in my mouth and bit on it lightly. He let out a mild groan.

We got all of our foot coverings off and I unzipped my jeans and let them fall. I wasn't wearing underwear and my nuts hit the air gratefully, while my dick opened out like a fat knife. I was uncut and the head started to throb. I wanted to prolong this and not shoot all over his clean, ironed sheets in ten seconds. He pulled down his pinstriped pants. He was wearing

55

nice, designer-type bikini undershorts that actually showed off his beautiful rump. The bulge under them was more than obvious.

I pulled him over to me and ran my tongue on top of his basket, that was pressing hard to be released. His dick uncoiled like a thick snake in a bag. I took my time running my mouth over the silky, cotton shorts, till I got them very wet and could feel the heat from his cock under them.

Then I pulled them off him. I came close to ripping them, which didn't bother me at all. I made him stand up over me while I sucked his dick like an ice cream pop. He was thick and uncut, but with a magnificent head on it and very little overhang. The foreskin felt as silky as his sheets, his underwear, as everything about him. His ass was baby-ass smooth, even silkier, but there was a fine powdering of ash-blond hair just above it, at the small of his back. I turned him around and started running my tongue through the hair, then into his asshole, which tasted great. While I did that, I kept one hand on his cock, which throbbed in my hand, so that I could feel the blood jump in it.

"You've got to stop," he told me. I didn't want to stop, so I pulled him down forcefully and made him sit on my cock, while I sat on the edge of his pretty bed.

"Why?" I asked. "Why stop now?" He smiled again, then closed his eyes. We were both too hot to last very long, but I pulled his legs out, and bent over him, sucking his long, silken meat, while I butted my dick into him more.

A couple of minutes later, while I was licking his tits, as we were both recovering from an almost simultaneous orgasm, I wondered why we should stop. "I wanted to make it last longer," he explained. "So we'll do it again," I said.

I fucked him once more, and then left. I gave him my telephone number and took his. I felt funny about calling him, though. I was living in a rat trap in the East Village, one of those places people like Devlin Hanson would find quaint and then try to find a cab out of as soon as possible. I was also, frankly, not all that interested in other people's money. I'd had money before and lost it and known people with money. Maybe I had a bad feeling about the rich, that they cared more about impressing you than staying with you. So, in short, I couldn't see myself fawning all over Devlin, and I had a feeling that was what was expected.

That Friday, though, I got a call from him, around noon, while I was working on a story. "Can you meet me in mid-town this afternoon. About five? I'll get off early."

I told him I was busy and wanted to know why? "I've got some shopping I want to do. Do you know where Cartier's is? Next to Cartier's is another jewelry shop I like. I'll tell you the address ..."

I told him I was busy. As much as I liked everything about him physically, I was not going to be impressed by Devlin while he spent money. Then he asked me several times more, and actually he sounded like this was so important—he was pleading (ah ... the helpless rich!). Anyway, I gave in.

This time I wore what was left of my preppy wardrobe—loafers, button-down shirt, a V-neck sweater in a *tasteful*, creamy color; cord jeans. I got to the store early. There was a snotty, European-queen clerk who met me at the door. I told him I was waiting for Mr. Hanson. He became nicer and offered me a cup of coffee, which I took while I looked at the goodies in the black cases. The place had real "ice," as Damon Runyon would say. Diamonds definitely are a girl's best friend, and probably wouldn't hurt most boys. In other words, I could have lived very nicely—for a very long time—on what was in one wristwatch case alone.

Dev arrived out of breath. He was sorry to be late, but he had a hard time finding a cab. The clerk escorted us upstairs. "Ze special room," he said. Dev winked at me and we went up a narrow flight of stairs.

The clerk switched on a light and took a black, satin pillow out of a safe. I still had no idea what was going on. "Ees zees what we are talking about, Meester Hanson?" he said. The pillow was piled with tiny rings, from less than a quarter inch in diameter to about half an inch. He scooped up several and showed them to us. "Zees are very special. Zay are *platinum*."

Dev looked at them. He picked up a few and felt their weight.

"Would you like to try?" the clerk said. "I will leave the room. I trust you ..."

Dev nodded and the clerk left. By the time I put two and two together, Dev had unzipped his trousers and pulled his cock out. He was excited by the scene and almost hard. "I want it to go right here," he explained to me, and put one of the rings at the tip of his foreskin.

I looked seriously and thought about it. "Maybe it should go right here," I said, and put the same ring a little lower, so that it would go straight through, just below where his foreskin rolled over the large, plum-like head.

"That would be harder," he said. "Two holes."

"Well, I'm sure we can find a doctor who'll do it."

He shook his head. "No, I want you to do it."

A minute later, the clerk came back in. "I'll take this one." Dev pointed to the heavier, half-inch platinum.

We got into a cab to go over to his apartment. I was getting nervous. "Don't worry," Dev said. "I know what I'm doing. I was a medic in the Army. I've helped take people's arms off."

"Why didn't you become a doctor?" I asked.

"There wasn't enough money in it," he smiled. "Look, I've got everything we need at home, including some spray-on anesthetic. It'll deaden the area completely."

As we approached Beekman Place, he took the small, velvet covered, jeweler's box out of his cashmere overcoat pocket. He flipped it open. The platinum glowed softly. "It's a beauty, isn't it?"

I had admit my nerves increased by the time we got past his doorman, and the elevator boy who kept whistling (of all things!) "Blue Velvet," and the three stairs to his living room. I was close to a wreck. I tried hard not to show it, but Dev must have sensed it because I kept breaking into a barking nervous kind of laughter. When we sat down on the couch, I looked up at the gilt mirror over the mantle piece. My tense smile looked very familiar: I'd seen it on Dev's face that first evening in the Yukon.

"Relax, don't worry," Dev said and got up. "Let me get you a drink. He poured me a finger of cognac in a large brandy snifter. I drank some of it, and he opened his mouth and started to lick the cognac off my lips with his tongue. Then we started passing small swallows of it back and forth. It became a game. I loosened up and soon we were out of all of our clothes. I became extremely hot for him, and his dick started to throb with expectation. I grabbed at his ass, and took the lower, thick part of his cock in my hands, drawing him nearer to me.

"Whoa," he said, and gently pushed me off. "I want to do this first."

We were both naked; he led me innocently by the hand into his bathroom. It was large and outfitted with a lot of black porcelain that was supposed to look like marble. "You're going to have to wash your hands really well," he said and pulled out a plastic bottle of surgical prep soap. I used it on my hands, getting as deeply under my fingernails as I could.

"Okay," he said. "Now put these gloves on." He popped a pair of skin-tight surgical gloves out of a plastic bag and handed them to me. I had a hard time getting them on. I was getting nervous again. The cognac wore off and my cock started to shrivel.

"Now this is what we're going to do," he told me calmly, and he explained that the ring had a small opening where its diameter narrowed. I was going to pierce the tip of his foreskin with a disposable I.V. needle—the type used to introduce liquids into patients, not the type used for general injections. Once I got the needle through the foreskin, Dev would insert the tiny, thinner stem at the opening of the ring into the I.V.'s hollow point; then once the stem was firmly in the needle, we'd pull it back through his foreskin.

"Do you understand?" he asked me firmly. "If you don't, I'll repeat it again." I nodded my head rather blankly, and hoped that—under what was becoming real panic—I did understand what he was saying. He then washed his hands and his complete "genital area" very well, and took a can of spray-on anesthetic out of his medicine cabinet and sprayed it liberally on his foreskin and most of the shaft of his cock.

"How does it feel?" I asked him.

"Cold. Cold and kind of dead."

He handed me the needle, sterilized in a cellophane wrapper, and I managed to crack it open. My hands shook. I had once given a diabetic friend of mine his injection, but I had never done anything like this. Dev looked at me like he expected to have this thing done for him. "Well ...?" he said.

I sat down on the vinyl toilet seat cover, which felt cool and almost calming, and then poised the I.V. needle at the place on his foreskin he'd pointed to. I was afraid my hands were really trembling. I broke out into a cold sweat and wondered why I'd gotten myself into this ... why *he'd* gotten me into it. Then I closed my eyes, and jabbed the damned needle through.

He didn't flinch. I opened my eyes and saw that the needle had pierced his foreskin; for a moment there was no blood. Then Dev handed me the ring, and I put the thin stem of it into the opening of the I.V.

Now, carefully, I was supposed to draw it back through the hole in Dev's foreskin.

"Are you okay? he whispered to me, gently.

I told him I was and nervously asked how he was. He said he was fine. There was some pain, but not as much as he'd expected. He told me as long as the needle was in his foreskin, there'd be no blood.

Then I began to draw the I.V. needle back out, hopefully inserting the ring completely through his foreskin at the same time. I held my breath while I did it. The stem went into the pierced hole, and was almost "home," when suddenly this tiny filament of platinum fell out of the needle's opening. "Jesus!" I shrieked.

"We're going to have to do it again," he said, quite coolly.

I exhaled slowly and tried to calm myself. He came closer to me and put his lips on my mouth. I knew my lips felt like ice. "I don't think I can do it," I told him. The fear that I was inflicting too much pain on him was killing me. Then I realized something; that maybe situations like these caused men to fall in love with each other.

He smiled. "Don't worry. Go into the living room for a minute. Maybe you should lie down on the rug."

I got up and looked at myself in the bathroom mirror. I was as white as a sheet. I managed to get to the living room, and then stretched out on his Chinese rug. A moment later, I fell asleep. I felt so tired that I wasn't even sure that I hadn't fainted.

I woke up what seemed like hours later. In fact, it was only about five

59

minutes. Dev was sitting next to me on the rug. We were still naked and he felt so warm and delicious that I wanted to suck every inch of him again. I began kissing him. "Whoa, boy," he said to me. "Don't get me too excited for a minute. Do you want to see it?"

He skinned back his foreskin a bit. There, buried under the delicate fold, was the ring, beautifully drawn through the tip of his foreskin.

I couldn't believe that he'd done it by himself. "You did all the hard stuff," he told me. I didn't believe him. "You did. Once the hole was there, it was easy to draw it through again. I'll have to be careful with it the next couple of days. I have a doctor who'll take care of any infections, but I think tonight I'm going to have to let this part just rest a bit."

I smiled. We had some more cognac, found something to eat in his refrigerator, and then fell asleep together in his bed.

I saw a lot more of Dev. It was truly one of those weird things: it was hard for me to comfortable around him, but I was attracted to him anyway. He reminded me of a lot of rich men I'd known. He could make life very exciting for you, but then you started to hate yourself for giving into his games, his self-importance. There were several times when I was with him that I felt close to exploding. He could keep you waiting for an hour, and always came in with a wonderful excuse and a lot of charm. I knew also that he had to be patient with me. I couldn't spend on his level, and I didn't come from his preppy background where you could just wave off anything. Dev never showed me that he was hurt, or bothered, and I started to see how he hid behind that wild smile of his a lot of problems.

After several months, I felt things getting more distant, more difficult between us. It was then that I realized that we just didn't want to hurt each other, so I stopped calling him.

Then I started seeing Pete, a young "performance" artist I'd met in a place called the Bar in the East Village. He was ten years younger than me, with a fresh face and a vanilla ice cream body I had few intentions of getting enough of. Dev called me a few times. He was always busy, but he'd call anyway. Finally, I told him very coldly that if he was calling me to tell me he was too busy to see me, there were other people who weren't. He hung up.

I thought about calling him back, but didn't. I felt shitty about myself; worse than I'd felt in a long time. I went over to see Pete that night and told him I wanted to see more of him. He told me he'd think about it.

Two days later, in the late afternoon, when I normally worked, somebody buzzed my intercom. I thought it was Pete and got excited. I asked who it was. It was a special delivery messenger. I signed for a small, well-packed cardboard box. Inside was a tiny, black velvet jeweler's box. I opened that. Inside, was a small platinum ring. Under it was one of Dev's business cards. I flicked it around. On the other side, it read: "For you, I'm never too busy."

With a little luck, I managed to scrape together the money and took a cab uptown. This time, Dev's doorman did not ignore me.

THE FROG POND

I had been trying not to look at him, or at least not to *let* him know I'd been looking at him for about ten minutes. You wonder sometimes why you play those kind of games with guys, especially when you go out looking for sex to begin with. I admit it; I had. Then he put his beer down on a convenient ledge opposite the bar, and walked up to me. "Would you be embarrassed if I said to you I wanted your dick now?" he asked.

I exhaled and started to smile. "No," I whispered.

"Good."

I nodded my head. Alright, these kind of things can just drop in your lap. If you're lucky. I had been looking right at him, across the bar. And it had been that kind of day: New Orleans. Middle of June. Hot. Sticky. So steamy you felt that the Mississippi itself was running its course right through town. But sometimes you want to bless those days, when the air in New Orleans gets so hot and wet that it's absolutely juicy with sex. And it is very available if you know where to look.

I turned slightly on the high wooden bar stool to get a better look at him. I was sure I could tell everything about him, just by looking at him. Have you ever felt that way, just by looking for a few seconds at a guy? He was about medium height, with a huge, broad, working man's build. Probably,

63

he'd been recently promoted to manager after working on oil rigs most of his life. I could see that part of his history even through the white office shirt and skinny black tie he wore. The blue collar was showing right behind the white. He might work in an office, but you could never get the smell of oil, salt, and sand off him. And probably he'd just come in straight from his office somewhere off Poydras Street. A lot of guys did that: they'd stop off in the French Quarter bars, grab a cocktail at happy hour, some cool air, and then look for something hot. Anything hot.

I went on looking at him, while he grinned at me.

He was about thirty-five. Reddish, coarse hair, cropped short. Also, a reddish, closely cropped beard and mustache. Thin blue eyes. Quiet blue, deep blue, but thin. A blue like chalk. Like blueberry soda. Cool blue eyes; the eyes I'd seen on Van Gogh paintings of men; the kind of eyes that if you were looking for a hot man, you couldn't turn away from. He had a heavy jawbone, and a large, "Dutch" kind of nose. He was a good-looking man— not "pretty"; I wasn't interested in pretty—but good looking. And even better, he was the type who didn't know he was good-looking.

Frankly, I like that. They're the only type worth going after.

"Why're you looking so hard at me?" he asked. "I know. I don't come on worth a shit, do I? You probably think I'm nuts."

"No, I don't," I reassured him. I ran my hand down the front of his white shirt. It was already sopping wet with perspiration. Air conditioning just wasn't enough today. It only cooled the air; it didn't dry it out. PawPaws, my bar, was always dark, like some ancient Egyptian temple on the edge of the Nile. With one hand, I started to unbutton the oyster buttons on his cotton shirt. The shirt was handkerchief thin. I slipped my fingers in and felt his muscular, hairy, red chest. The hairs felt wiry; pleasant. I could feel heavy drops of sweat running off those red hairs, like water running off iron rust—over his ribs, his muscles. My hand found one of his nipples. It was thick; meaty; already getting hard. Slightly pointy. I wanted to ask if he lived close by. He jumped me to the gun.

He didn't. He lived across the Mississippi in one of the outer, suburban parishes, where the houses spread out, and sometimes boats came up to your backyard. "It's a long story," he said. I didn't ask anymore. I've never been one to interfere with a long story.

I took another pull from my beer. My tongue instinctively licked the foam off my mustache. It was funny: I could tell I was turning him on as much as he did the same thing to me. Sometimes these things work; other times they don't. I wasn't sure if I wanted to take him home, though. A friend of mine from New York, Darrell, was staying with me at my small place in the Quarter. We had a non-proliferation trick pact. He didn't on me; I didn't on him. I didn't want to impose on Darrell, who was probably home sleeping off the night before. My place down the street was just big enough for a set of dishes, a set of sheets, and a couple of cockroaches. So I wasn't sure what to do with gorgeous Red here. I didn't want to make Darrell clear out, even to cool my urgent desires. I'm not the sort of host who "imposes" on his guests.

I took another swig from the beer. It was now about six-thirty, and just as hot as ever outside. More men started coming in. I knew some of them. They called over to me. Because PawPaws is on Burgundy Street and away from the Bourbon Street tourist traps, it's a friendlier bar, and not so queeny or cliquey. At a lot of New Orleans bars, you can't go two minutes without being hit by a screaming "Miss Thang!!!" siren-call whistling through the air. Then Miss Thing herself comes trumping down on you, screaming "Where you been, Sugar-plum???" It ruins any sense of concentration you have. But at PawPaws, we were more relaxed. The cliental thought a canapé was something like a corn doodle, and the bar staff could not be trusted with any drinks beyond rum-and-Coke. But this suited me fine. If I wanted a good martini, there were other places for that.

"I gotta pee," the man said. There was a good bulge in his damp chinos. I recognized a piss hard. He leaned over to me, and whispered above the din of conversation and disco: "Want me to suck you in the men's room?"

My throat went dry. My heart started to pound. These were all good signs. I did want him, but the question was how much? The answer came to me straight from my own body: A lot. But I wasn't ready for so much, so soon. I closed my eyes. "I'll think about that," I answered, trying to be a cool shit.

"Don't think too hard," he answered, and I saw him move past a group of four guys at the other end of the bar, towards the men's john. They were all wearing Levi's, with tight, hot bodies. Two were bare chested, something never discouraged in this bar. I wondered suddenly why this guy wanted me. I'm not at all bad looking—but sometimes, well—we all wonder that. The more I questioned it, the more I decided that I should follow him. After all, only he could give me the answer.

I have a good body. I work out a lot, but I don't show it off the way some men do. I feel embarrassed. I love to look at hot men with as little clothes on as possible, but I feel embarrassed by my own nakedness in front of others. I also feel embarrassed by my own horniness. Maybe that comes from our repressed upbringing, being made to feel that it's frivolous. You can be hungry, but not horny, as if hunger for sex isn't a hunger that really matters.

But I admit, there are times when I enjoy horniness. I love it. I've never been one of those "professional gays" who wear all the right clothes, the right hankies in the right pockets, hair trimmed perfectly, who seem to live just from one trick to the next. I've never been like that, but it's still hard for

65

me to admit how much I want a man sometimes.

A moment later, I followed him.

I closed the door to the small men's room. It had only one toilet and was just big enough for two, especially if they were both busy with each other's cock. He was just about ready to put his back in, when he saw me. "Hi there," he said, and flipped it casually back out, like he was showing off a key chain, or something like that. It was really pretty short, but very, *very* thick. The veining on it was also thick, and reminded me of the veining on a good runner's ankles. The head was deep red and flattened out like the snout of a pit bull. Although he was uncut, he had rolled it back. I could tell that he—for some reason red-headed guys always seemed to—kept his meat clean. I couldn't help leaning over and putting my left hand around the base of it.

His knob felt warm, like a new light bulb that had just been snapped on. With my hand on it, it got hotter.

"Baby," he whispered. "That feels good."

I didn't want to say anything. I was starting to vibrate all over the way I do when I get excited, when I know sex is just around the corner. I started, almost unconsciously, to pull up my tee shirt, wet with all that damn sweat, and he ran his big, hairy hands over my chest. I was sunburned dark, with almost no chest hair. My chest felt like spaghetti when it comes straight out of the pot, with hot, running water all over it. Suddenly, I was enjoying this heat.

"I'd like to get *real* naked with you," he said.

"Real naked?" I asked. The idea was very, *very* exciting.

He nodded his head, and the thick reddish curls caught the light. His hair had an authentic pubic quality.

"Sounds wonderful," I said, as more saliva came to my throat. Somehow, he managed to shove that stiff, thick dick of his into his Jockeys, and pulled up his chinos. We closed the door to the men's room and went back into the bar. Several pairs of eyes went over to me, but nobody said a thing. I ordered another beer in a plastic go-cup from Roger, my favorite bartender, and tipped him half a buck. "Thanks heaps, luv," Roger called out to me, as I took the beer out the door with me. Roger could stretch out "luv" until it reached half way around the block, and I heard it even after the two of us had cleared the door of the bar.

It was now dark outside, that premature darkness of a New Orleans summer thunder shower. The air was so heavy with this shower—already well on its way—that you could stuff a meat grinder with it.

"Where we gonna go?" he asked. "My car's over there." He pointed down the block to a light blue Datson compact, almost, but not quite, the color of his eyes.

I hesitated for a moment. I was in a quandary myself. We got into his car, just as the sky opened up. July showers were like that. It would be buckets for about half an hour; then it would clear, although it wouldn't get much cooler. I told him to go straight up Burgundy Street and he drove through the old Quarter, until we passed Esplanade Avenue, a beautiful broad street lined with huge live oak trees on both sides. A middle "neutral ground" favored by joggers and dog walkers—two groups very mutually antagonistic—was also planted with oaks, so that in a storm Esplanade seemed more like a grove in the country than a city street. But New Orleans was like that: suddenly you'd come to a back yard or a grove of trees and swear that the country had reclaimed everything. On some streets banana trees grew as thick as in Honduras.

We drove on a bit further and turned left. A friend of mine was sharing a large, broken down "historic" house in a section called Bywater. The house was from the 1840s and was big enough for a Napoleonic regiment. At one time it had belonged to the overseer of a plantation when huge plantations still existed in that part of the city.

David, my friend, had told me that most of the other tenants had left for the summer. The place was really too broken down for real renting—there was little plumbing and you could forget the heat in New Orleans' brief but blood-chilling winters. The owner of the place, a crazy old lady from the Garden District named Mrs. Mingledorf, was waiting either to die or sell it. Since restoration would cost much more than the house, it was easier to rent out rooms, or groups of rooms to whomever needed the space and could put up with the inconveniences. David had been there for three years, and was now official ringmaster of the "Mingledorf Mansion," as it was called. He simply sent the old lady a monthly rent check based on the occupancy of the house.

We parked the car outside a stand of bamboo that shaded the Mansion from the road. It had let up for a few minutes and now it was pouring again. "What's your name?" he asked me, then leaned over and kissed me on the mouth before I could answer. His mouth tasted the way I like men to taste—fresh, with undertones of whiskey and good cigarettes (you don't get that taste from smoking Carltons; it's an unfiltered Camel taste). When I came up for air, he told me his. His name was Grayson, and he sounded so southern and truthful then that I'm sure it was his name. We locked the car and then tore through the path between bamboo stands and sheets of rain for at least a hundred feet, to the house.

We literally crashed onto the veranda—the front porch—and I banged on the large double doors. I used a heavy brass knocker in a strange design. It was a hand holding a child's foot. David told me that these odd knockers were traditional on old New Orleans homes, the idea was that they protected children from fevers.

I used the knocker for several minutes. I was hot-sexy and hot-steamy from being in the car with Grayson. He was soaked through. His crotch bulged like neon sign that said: "Play With This." I felt really frustrated. The Mansion was empty. Locked and empty.

"Shit, it's locked," I said. My face fell. I was sure David would be home. I had brought guys to his house before in tight circumstances.

"There's nobody here?" Grayson asked.

I nodded my head yes.

"Who the fuck cares?" he said and started to peel off his shirt. His chest hairs were stuck by the rain to his chest, and as soon as he unbuttoned his shirt, I ran my tongue all the way down his upper body to his salty navel.

"Let me," I offered, and unbuckled his belt. I flapped open his wet chinos. His dick was ready to stand at attention inside his Jockeys. My mouth found the thick, meaty head of it as soon as I pulled his undershorts down.

"Let me take my shoes off," he said, and he clumsily managed to get them off without falling on his face.

I kneeled down on the old wooden floor boards and started working his cock with my mouth, while I fingered his large, muscular butt cheeks. They were as hard and round as two cantaloups, perfectly formed and ripened. It was the kinds of man-body I liked—not the skinny, shiny, puffy cheeks of some kid who's just off baby powder. His dick, which was very responsive to me, started to throb in my mouth as I worked on the full head of it.

"Let's get out of the rain," he said. I could tell he was so hot and horny-fearless that he could have sucked off a horse on Bourbon Street. New Orleans in the summer had a way of doing that to you, releasing every inhibition, especially in the naturally uninhibited.

We finished peeling off all of our wet clothes, and I pointed him towards the back of the old house. We hurried barefoot down a cobblestone walkway. The stones felt slick as spit under our feet, with mud oozing up between each hard mound. The rain suddenly picked up again. It came down in thick sheets, so that you could hardly see your hand in front of you.

In the back was a large, empty stable that had gone through several different conversions. At one time it had been a tool shed, a garage, a very rustic guest cottage, and finally what it was now: a sculptor's studio. It was two stories high with no windows on the first story, but a large sky light on the second. The light inside was a soft, pearly gray. David was also a sculptor, mostly in wood. He kept his wood pieces under several large tarpaulins of heavy canvas. I unrolled some of the canvas on the floor, and then pulled Grayson down on it.

His stocky body warmed me while shoved his thick organ into my mouth. We had gone past the thinking part, and were now like two pigs in heat. I got him hotter and hotter, and he started to groan a slow, deep moan of sheer appreciation. Then he took his cock out of my mouth and started sucking on me; we soon found ourselves mutually satisfying each other while I probed his asshole with my fingers. Then I realized what I wanted to do.

I quit sucking his peter for a moment, and pulled myself away from his warm, hungry mouth. I put my hand around his large, excited hairy balls. It as a nice feeling—just pulling him, ever so gently by his balls. They were in a flesh sack that felt almost leathery, like I imagined the skin of a calf elephant's belly felt.

"Where you wanna go?" he asked. His cool blue eyes, half closed, looked at me.

I remembered that on the other side of the studio was an old square shallow pond lined with marble slabs. It had been there forever and was now choked with small water lily pads. The water was oozy and warm, tropical. Primal. Like thick piss.

"Just some place," I said, and we walked outside naked. The rain had completely stopped. The air was steamy and thick again. Although it was now dark in the courtyard, I knew exactly where the pond was.

"You wanna go in that pond?" he asked me. He scratched his thick red hair and then started swirling the red hair on his belly into inviting patterns. I nodded my head. He smiled. I could tell he was game.

We slid slowly down into the water. It smelled green and primitive, a succulent, thick smell you associated with living matter. It was slightly warmer than the close air. There were no crocodiles, no snakes; only a few small jade-green frogs that jumped in and out, hardly noticing us. Suddenly, I felt that this must have been the way humans began on Earth, wading through soupy, primitive waters, hunting fish and frogs, leaving the water in a state of sexual heat. The pond came only up to Grayson's thighs, and I started sucking his dick again in the warm water. He let out a full, sub-human, ape-like groan of pleasure.

After a few minutes, when I had had enough of his dick, I turned him around and moistened the chute of his ass with my saliva.

He opened up quickly for me and leaned his chest against the slick, marble side of the pond. The warm water licked gently at my balls and even slide into the slick walls of his manhole. I held his waist tightly, running my hands into his wet, thick red chest fur. I squeezed his nipples. They were already large and thick like plums. After a couple of soft, smooth strokes deep inside him, I felt very united with this stranger I'd met only a short while ago in the bar. Now we were in this dark, exciting setting that drifted towards us directly out of old New Orleans. The courtyard was so quiet—

69

hushed—like some other movement was going to begin any second, but didn't quite dare. Time had stopped it. All I could hear were large drops of water rolling off a huge magnolia tree and Grayson's heavy breathing as his strong ass muscles moved with my cock.

"Sure feels good," he said. "Jus' stay a little longer."

I complied willingly, while he brought himself off. I saw thick white gobs of jism floating on the green water. The wandering leaves of a few lily pads caught some of it. The jism looked like beads of ivory. In another month the lilies, little blue and white ones that looked like spiky bells, would open. Their fragrance would spread through the whole courtyard.

Grayson was completely relaxed now. I turned him around, so that he was sitting back on my cock, facing away from me. I leaned back on the marble tiles, and held him close to me with my dick inside him. The both of us hardly moved or breathed. Then I pulled out of him and jerked myself off into the water, too.

I blanked out then; I was that satisfied by what had happened there in the frog pond with him. When my eyes opened again, I saw that the moon had appeared over the magnolia tree, and that Grayson had pulled himself up out of the pond.

I got out then, and saw him naked, standing against the side of David's studio. A few drops of fresh sperm glistened like dew on his cock head, which just peered out of his foreskin. My mouth went down hungry on it. I was sorry now that the frog pond had taken most of his cum.

Our clothes stank. They felt wet and cold, but we managed to get them back on. David still didn't appear—I wanted to show Grayson the inside of the Mingledorf Mansion, it still had its original staircase, and a fabulous ballroom with its original wallpaper. But the house was locked, so we got back into his Datson.

"That's sure one beautiful old house," Grayson said as he started the motor. I agreed that it was. He smiled and looked at me. "I will never forget that house. Or that pond. Where do you want me to drop you off?" he asked.

SEX & VIOLENCE

A CINEMATIC SHORT, SHORT STORY

Every place that my lips touched his body, I wanted it to burn slightly; to smoke.

"You glitter, you know?" I said. "You really glitter."

He did. Perspiration glittered off him in the lamplight, from his smooth back and then down onto his legs. He seemed covered in dark honey. I stroked him all the way down his back, to the white creases in the bend of each knee.

"Sex, okay?" I asked nervously.

"Sure," he answered. "I want to have sex with you. You know that." He turned towards me and picked up my cock from where it rested by his hand, in the wild strands of a Greek goatskin rug. It sprang to life, getting very hard as his fingers moistened the tip with his saliva. He placed my fingers in his mouth. It was very warm; each finger ran a velvet circle around his tongue. He guided them in, one by one, and finished with the thumb.

I turned him on his stomach and greased his ass, then carefully pushed my dick into him. He was used to much rougher stuff. "You don't have to be so light. I'm not an old lady."

I agreed and really—as they say—let him have it. It was wonderful letting go inside of him. I came in great hot jets. He could feel me rumbling

71

through him like a volcano jacking off into an ocean. He only cooled me down, but did not quench me. I sucked him off hungrily. I wanted to eat each hair on his prick, and ran my tongue down along the groove of that vein on the inner side of his penis until the vermillion tip of it hurt.

He tasted like rainwater, distilled and thickened. I had to pee. I got up and put my hand up to his mouth. "Don't move," I joked with him. "I'll be right back. Scout's honor."

I stayed hard even over the bowl. I almost had to squat to aim right. My legs shook a bit from excitement. If he was mine—if that was possible—I would keep him in my eyes—in my mind—as if he was a rare jewel, a diamond pinned right through my throat. I heard some noise near the door. It was probably my neighbors, I thought. God, they were a noisy bunch. I peed quickly and then heard a car backfire like a hard slap, in the front of the building. When I returned to the living room where he was lying on the flotaki, I saw two hoods leaning over him.

One of them turned to me. He wore a black raincoat pulled all the way up to his nose. A gray driving hat covered his brow. All I could see was a dark hole suggesting a face. "Don't come any closer," he warned. "We don't get a bonus for two."

They charged out the door, while I stood, naked and dazed, and watched them. The door slammed.

I dove into him—and jumped back. They had blown a great deal of his head off. My stomach could hardly hold it. I became dizzy. What would the cops say: me, naked, blacked out over the body?

Seconds later, I cooled off—then threw a bathrobe over him. I didn't want him to leave my house so soon. I pulled on some pants and found a shirt. There was nothing for me to carry in the house, but I remembered that my neighbor kept a small revolver in his desk in his living room. It was kept next to his important papers—his divorce decree, some stock certificates and his gym membership. He was in the Hamptons for the weekend, and I was supposed to feed his cat. The cat was very glad to see me. I found some small cans on the redwood counter in the kitchen, scooped out something that must have come from some animal, and then went through the desk.

The "Inferno" as its name implied, was the disco of the Damned. It was huge, with many layers and rooms. Although the morning sun was edging its way onto the horizon of the City, it still wasn't too late for the crowd of guys who hung out outside and in it. The music was venomous. It was a habit like heroin: leaching brain matter itself. It ran through your blood and packed your head for days, ringing back and forth, finally settling into your dreams. They were disco dreams: you'd do the same thing over and over, night after night. There was a dance in this dream, with no movement, just drifting in patterns on the floor. I paid some money to a large man at the door to get in. He took the money mechanically. I realized I was there because of the smoke in the air. I could hardly breathe; asthma troubles since childhood. I asked the door goon where Mr. Crewe was. "He's in the back. Whatcha want him for?"

"I'm a friend of Takey's. John Takey."

"That one—him? He left Crewe, y' know? Crewe didn't go for that one bit."

"I've got a message from Takey."

"How could you have a message for Mr. Crewe. Mr. Crewe never takes messages from the Dead."

"How do you know Takey's dead?" I asked.

"He might as well be. They leave and then they try to come back. But Crewe don't want 'em back. So he treats 'em like they was dead. I'll take you to Crewe. You can talk to him yourself."

Mr. Crewe was in the back room with two of his goons. A slender young boy walked in, handed Mr. Crewe a cup of coffee, and walked out. They continued watching the floor on closed circuit monitors. I wanted Crewe to myself. "You a friend of Takey?" he asked me. I nodded. "Nice boy, he was."

"Was?" I asked.

"He left."

"But I hear they come back," I said.

"Not Takey."

"Why not?"

He spit some of the smoke from his black cigar into my face. "How the fuck should I know? He was different."

"Very different," I said, and pulled the pistol out from the pocket of my leather jacket.

Crewe did not blink. "Why don't you put that thing down before one of my boys makes Crewe-stew out of you?" He smirked at me.

My jaw hardened. "I want to blow your brains out like you did Takey," I said.

"Do you think I'd waste a contract on a little punk like him?"

I could hardly hold back any longer. My hand started shaking; I wanted to squeeze the trigger so hard I could taste the gunpowder in the back of my mouth. I just wanted to be done with all of this. Crewe saw my nerves twitch.

"They've sent a queen to do a man's work," Crewe said to me blandly.

"Shut up, asshole," I shouted. He could see the shakes I was going through, so I added, butch as possible: "Or I'll clean out your pipes from the top drawer."

His men had now edged behind me. I either had to sink their boss to the floor—or I wouldn't be able to finish the next sentence. They had the drop on me, and both Crewe and I knew it.

Crewe threw his head back on his thick neck. He was balding and tanned; his face half Rome and half Boston, like a mixture of olive oil and whiskey. He smiled right at me, and then told it to me: "It was his *father*. I knew the sonovabitch, colonel in the Army. Irish Catholic, heavy example of the breed, if you know what I mean? Funny, I'm Catholic and I screw boys and I don't go bonkers over it. The old man knew John was working here— he came over acting like he was going to get the Senate after me. Shit, we've had Vice Presidents in here. Well, one Vice President. I admit he didn't last that long. Anyway, kiddo, it was his old man. Just couldn't deal with it, the old 'My son the faggot' routine. Jesus, how that bores me. That's the best I can say for it. It bores me. Why can't they ever learn? Listen boys (I lowered my gun; I knew he was telling the truth. You don't laugh at a man when a gun's pointing at you, unless you're telling the truth): Let this gentleman out of here nice. He's had a hard blow to himself. Come back soon, another time. Tell 'em Mr. Crewe knows you. They'll let you in."

I left. The evening just collapsed, airless, around me. I got outside, and felt my stomach aching for something: stress did that for me. I grabbed myself a cup of coffee and a jelly doughnut in a diner frequented by leather boys with dyed blond hair in motorcycle jackets. I looked around both sides of the counter. None of these guys seemed real, and I remembered how nice Takey's dick felt in my mouth. I smiled: it was funny, I thought, how little substance our life contains. People die as suddenly in real life as they do in the movies. Or was it the other way around? Who can explain it? I wasn't crazy about sadism. I used to turn away from the screen at the sight of pain, but I know writers are not like other people: we bleed deeper.

I looked up Takey's name in the phone book. I hadn't expected to find it, but there it was, in fine print, black and white. He was drunk when he answered the phone. "I'm sorry to be this way," he slobbered. "I'm not used to drinking. You tell me you want to talk about my son? Sorry, Mister, but I don't want to talk about him."

"Then he might as well be dead," I said, lighting a cigarette in the phone booth. It was very late—I admit it—and I wondered what the hell I was doing there out in the morning damp, while John Takey lay almost headless in my apartment. It was hell on my asthma, that dampness. And I knew I shouldn't be smoking, but it was true, nicotine did calm nerves. "Can I see you tonight?" I said to the old man. "About John?"

"I told you I didn't want to talk about him."

"Then change your fucking mind," I said, and hung up. I took a cab to his address. It was over by the river, not in a great part of town, but I had lost any sense of fear. The old man let me in himself. His place looked like it had never been lived in. Things were in boxes and filthy. The Colonel was obviously a pig: the sins of the fathers, I thought—that the sons should have to die for this. I was getting edgy again. Edgy and angry. I wanted to pull down the old man's pants and fuck him in his saggy ass. Then kill him. He handed me a glass of Scotch, filled like it was iced tea.

"You a faggot, too?" he asked, once I had sunk into a heavy chair covered in peeling fake horse hide.

"You put things so well."

"I didn't mean it that way. It's just that my son is."

"Is?"

"That's right. Unless he's gone over to the other side, he is. Listen, he's alright." He began to drool. "I loved the boy, I want you to know that."

"So did I."

"No, not that way, you didn't. You just wanted his dick." His face suddenly squeezed together like an old, dried apple. He did not approve of me, that was certain.

"I didn't love him your way," I said. "For me to love him, he had to be alive." I pulled out the gun and got to my feet. It had been him: I knew it. I could tell the way he looked at me. It was pure fear. Pure hatred. I had seen that look before, many times. "Where are your two goons!" I shouted.

"They aren't goons," he said calmly. His voice sounded like it was coming to me in bubbles, like he was speaking underwater.

"They killed your boy."

"You mean their brother," he said slowly.

"Jesus!" I screamed. Suddenly, I was crying the way *he* should have been. But there was no remorse in that sonovabitch. How could Takey have come from such a nest? The old man was passive like poison, like he would take the blame for nothing: everything had been caused by some other thing outside of himself. A war. Sex. His son's sex. The war against his son, John, and the men who were like him. We were so close when I pulled the trigger that the Colonel's brains splashed against the wall. The body fell back. I shot him several more times out of the purest rage: his neck looked like a severed pipe.

The boys bolted in from another room. I could tell they'd been sleeping, and were only half-dressed. They were both pasty looking, with faces like young vultures, bald heads and all. They screamed when they saw the old man's body. Then they saw me: "We'll get you! We'll get you yet!" they screamed at me. The screaming was like the cawing of carrion birds. They were all animals of filth, I decided.

I rushed past them, without saying another word. I went back to my apartment, and saw John's body again, just where I left it. Now, I was able to call the police. I told them that I'd passed out after I saw what happened. But I didn't get to see anything of his murderers: only their raincoats, and their eyes. "Must have been drugs," the detective said. "These things happen all the time." He filed a report and left.

I had to close off my apartment. I couldn't live in it anymore. The hearing was hideous; the newspapers got hold of the story, and my name and picture were plastered all over them. I was ready to commit suicide. But that only showed me who my friends were. A few stuck with me, but most split like flies after a flushing.

I was acquitted of any part in John Takey's death, and the Colonel's death was determined to be a suicide (five shots in the head?); sometimes I think it was the wrong decision, but I did not want to pay for the old man's death. I'd already paid enough for John Takey's.

I had to leave town. I took a plane for Lisbon. It seemed like a good place to dry out inside. On the plane I was afraid that any moment I would look across the aisle and see one of those pasty faces watching me. I started to think that I should have tried for something further. Tangier? Nepal? Malibu? One of those places where you can get lost and no one thinks to come after you. But I put a grip on myself. I ordered one of those canned cocktails from a stewardess, and slowly sipped it. The alcoholic warmth spread slowly through my body. I remembered John Takey's silky neck and stomach. My tongue ran over my lips, and I remembered his tongue in my mouth. I could taste his cock. I knew my life was starting over again. Soon my old life would be forgotten, washed away, like a package of old shirts loosely tied with string and dropped out of a plane over an ocean.

Dark Mouth

ᵾ

I know it was a strange situation: I'd meet Leeland every second Wednesday, around seven, at the baths. He'd come in from New Jersey, where he lived in Summit with his wife, whose name I'd never learned—or for that matter ever wanted to—and his kids, Jeff and Sally. He'd talk about the kids, but never about his wife. He was a strapping, fairly big guy, going just slightly—the kind of *slightly* I frankly like—to seed. That is, his stomach, which had been tight as a hardball, was getting a slight amount of gut to it; but the rest was hard. Even his hair was hard. It was hard, blond-orangy hair, kind of like the fur certain calico cats have, and it sprouted thick on top of his thirty-five-year-old head, and then covered his chest in thick, swirling patterns, the very memory of which makes me horny enough to want to start everything all over again with him.

The orangy hair tapered down in a regular "V" from his hard, almost pointy tits (that my teeth had gnawed to rawness during several Wednesdays), then pointed directly to his hard "outy" navel. The hair spread out again around his thick uncut wang, then brushed out from his large balls, and followed the deep orange crack of his ass, until it delta-ed out all over his ass-cheeks. His ass-cheeks were furry with cat-orange hair. His back had almost none on it, and his shoulders had a slight dusting on them.

He was the kind of man that queens would not find pretty. That is, to be more precise, I could not imagine Leeland's face and fanny in some spread in one of those Condé Naste magazines where the models have washboard stomachs and washboard faces to match. Leeland was real looking. His bottom lip was hard and still stuck out. His nose had a large bump on it, and he had a scar on his forehead from jumping into the ocean at Asbury Park and hitting some concrete that shouldn't have been there. This would not have happened on Fire Island or at Canne. But at Asbury Park, you couldn't always tell where the concrete was. His face and body had stories in them. He reminded me of a mountain that I wanted to climb. Once I got up there, I'd want to stick my dick in between certain warm rocks.

I did manage to stick my dick into him as much as possible. He liked to get fucked—an attraction he could not get from his wife—and that was part of the reason for our Wednesdays. He felt it was safer just to see one guy and the baths were a fairly safe place to do it. He did not want to come to my place. He did not want to get that involved with me, although I would have liked it—I *think* I would have liked it. Maybe a little bird tells me that it would have been smarter not to. My place, and I know I would have started making demands. Demands he couldn't have met. I'd met him at the baths, and we'd had one of those explosive, no-holds-barred sex scenes that make "promiscuity" its own reward. A kind of heat you can't get with a boyfriend. But any fool would get the idea that he did want to repeat it. So, afterwards, I offered him my phone number. He took it and called me a few days later. He said he could never see me at my house, so we set up the Wednesdays evenings when he must have made some excuse to his wife about something to do in the City.

At first, I wondered why he couldn't come to my place. I was living in Hell's Kitchen, in the West 50's, and he worked—so he told me—at least several times a week in the Broadway area, a couple of blocks away, in a new office building, when his company sent him into Manhattan. He made enough money to afford a hotel room, but to tell you the truth, I knew nothing about sneaking around. Wives have a way of going over your bills, so that might have shown up. But on the other hand, I think part of the come-on was keeping it at the baths—with all the sex going on around him. No hotel could compete with that. The sounds, the smells—even the air itself steamy and full of sex smells, like male asshole, shower soap, spray Lysol, poppers. For many men, that's a turn-on in itself. If you ever want to make a million dollars, just bottle a cologne called—well, you can call it whatever you want, but put in it the smell of male asshole, spray Lysol, shower soap, and stale poppers. I know I'll buy it and probably half of New Jersey will, too.

The first Wednesday we got together was kind of a tryout. We tried almost everything out. I must have rimmed him for about an hour. He loved it. He loved to talk dirty, while I worked my tongue through his gorgeous asshole. Sometimes I'd bite on the chunks of orange hair down there, then I'd suck on them, lick them, get them in my teeth, and then start all over again, just bearing my tongue down on in there.

He'd play with his own tits, twist them and pull them a bit, but he'd try not to beat his meat. The idea was that this was just a preliminary. Of course he got his fire engine hot, and after a while I'd get up and feel his nuts and the length of his shaft. They were all fever warm, trigger hot. Finally, I'd stick on a rubber and fuck him, while he called me "Fuckhead" and his "Asshole Eater." He told me these were two of his favorite words, but he couldn't use them in Summit. I think there were traffic rules against them: maybe they'd stop traffic.

The next couple of Wednesdays ran the same way. We'd meet at the baths. We'd get off on the idea that we'd actually planned to meet there. In effect, we were doing something "private," while everybody else outside the room—so we wanted to believe—was fucking and sucking more or less publicly.

Leeland was extremely hot, and frankly I think that almost anything I did to get him off would have worked. He had a real effect on me though. It made me bypass my usual reserve with guys and go directly into action. Maybe it was just his animal quality: the low, grunt noises he made; the words he used. I wondered how I'd been fortunate enough to find him, just by accident, and then was fortunate to get him back every other week.

Sometimes—I guess this is inevitable—I wondered if he ever "cheated" on me. It seems hard even to think about possessiveness in a situation like this, but possessiveness seems to be a human characteristic, so I know I had it, too. You can seriously try, but like sex, possessiveness is hard to get out of your system. So I wondered if he ever arrived early, just to trick around before the main event happened. (I did know that he left about 8:30 to get back to Summit and whatever her name was.) But I did wonder if he was *that* hot for other guys as well. I mean, it seemed hard to believe that he was just saving it up for me, twice a month. His wife might have been getting something, but we never, ever talked about that. I was curious though, and I wondered if he had a similar arrangement with some one else, maybe on a different day, maybe even at a different bath.

My curiosity finally got the better of me. That was about three months after we met, and I'd been thinking about Leeland a lot. I was starting to look forward more and more to those Wednesdays when we'd meet. So—let me just say out of sheer curiosity—our next Wednesday, I arrived earlier at the baths. I dashed for the steam room, hoping to see his orangy ass there, hoping to see it cutting through the hot vapors filled with guys on their knees and elbows, getting blown or fucked right after work. For some reason, 5:30 was always Get-Down-And-Do-It time in the steam room. I guess after being good all day, life must reserve some rewards.

I didn't see Leeland at all. Not a single orange hair of him. Instead, a slim, dark-headed, very Latino trick started coming on to me. His skin was silk smooth. He was shorter than me, but had a very hard chest and hard dick to go with it. His mouth though was a real miracle. It rolled all over my body, like a lubricated rubber ball, working its way into my sweat-soaked armpits, down my sides, and then around to my hard cock, which was panting and jerking with a force of its own, like my dick itself was breathing. My cock kept jerking up and down. There was no way I could hide that. I know much of this was because I was excited with the idea of seeing Leeland, here, in this sweat-soaked atmosphere. If I *had* caught Leeland in the steam room, red-handed, with a cock up his ass, I decided that I was going to suck his brains out right there.

Finally, "Ricardo" (my name for him; I decided that must be his name, whether he liked it or not) took my full meat in his mouth. I let him have it for a few hot seconds, but I knew that if I didn't get the hell out of there, in a minute I'd be drained and I didn't want to be that way for Leeland.

I shook myself loose of him. He was very attractive, dark, romantic. Alright, I admit sometimes I go south of all borders myself, but I knew then that I had to shower off and go back to my room, the room number that Leeland and I always arranged to meet in.

About ten minutes later, I was in the room, when I heard two knocks on the door. That was our signal. Two knocks, then two more. I got out of bed—with my pecker stuck out like a flag pole—and met him.

"Looks like you're ready," he said to me, with a broad, very approving smile on his face. Suddenly I felt—just looking at Leeland in the hazy, greenish light from the opened door of the room—that there was something almost mystical about him. He was so hot, so exciting to me, with his coarse, blond-orange hair and his rough looks. I think I could have just touched his body any place and gotten off. Maybe I was just primed too much from those few hot moments in the steam. But I felt like all my wires were out, and the electricity in the room when Leeland walked in could singe the hair off an orange cat.

"I'm ready," I told him. I took him into my arms and snapped the towel he wore—which just made it around his gut—off. He shut the door. For a moment, we were in total darkness while his hands scrambled all over me, and I could tell how hot he was, too. It was the kind of heat men who want men but have to wait for it feel. He suddenly tripped me with a quick, but not viscous, knee to my balls, and I flipped back on the bed, and he dove into me, biting and eating me, rutting like a pig at my tits, navel, and arm pits.

His mouth slurped all over me. I loved it. While he buried his face in my left pit, he kept saying, "You asshole shithead, you asshole shithead." I grabbed his thick, orangy hair and ran my fingers through it. Then I grabbed a handful of it, close to his scalp, and pushed his head down to my crotch so that I could stick my dick into his hair. The orange hairs prickled the head of my cock, like pure electrical sparks. His tongue took one of my balls and licked at it.

"Fuck you, shithead," he started saying. "Don't stick your dick in my hair. Stick it in my mouth, or up my ass."

I laughed and told him not yet. I knew I wasn't going to last more than a second if I tried to fuck him right then. I was too hot, too hot for my own good, maybe. My eyes were getting adjusted to the light, and frankly, I was getting more adjusted to just being hot there with him. It was a steady, ball-burning heat, and I didn't want to—I didn't even think I *could*, I was *that* hot—just get off right then, and go into the showers and start soaping what was left from his dick off me. I was hot and I wanted to coast on it. I wanted to fly around on it for a while more.

I wouldn't let him have my pecker, so he started rimming out my navel, which I love. There's a certain place, just above and then slightly below my bellybutton, that gets extremely excited, and his tongue and teeth started working on both places. I *wouldn't* let him get to my cock though. I held it back every time he grabbed for it. He swore at me, and started spanking my ass hard. Everytime he spanked me, I felt the light in the small cubicle flash in a different way. It was as if different, faint colors were coming out of it. I could also hear noises come in from outside; voices, but sometimes I thought I was hearing my own voice. It was like my brain, after heating up so much, was going into another channel. Perhaps it was just opening up to a new dimension that I had never experienced before. My body started to react, my muscles started jerking, while he found my tits again with his mouth, and rubbed his five o' clock orange shadow over my nipples and chest.

I knew I had to do something. I grabbed his hair again by his scalp, and pulled him up to me and pushed my mouth all the way into his mouth, like I was feeding him my whole head and face. I wanted him to swallow all of my teeth, my tongue, and lips. We rolled around on the narrow bed, and ended up on the floor. I knew we were on the floor because my head hit it with a hard bounce. The pain suddenly felt almost good. It brought me back—slightly at least—to some reality. I kept wondering why this Wednesday was so different from the others, why Leeland was so hot, so urgent.

81

He sat up for a moment, and leaned, dazed, against the mattress. I threw my head back and looked up at the ceiling, which seemed so far up above me as to be the sky. Usually, I didn't allow myself to think much when I was with a trick. It made things stickier. Leeland's life was his own business. But suddenly—maybe it was just the breather that I needed—I started to wonder what Leeland did the rest of the week. I knew that there was a certain button somewhere inside of me that allowed me to surrender most—if not all—of myself. Some men knew where that button was. I think every man has one; although some men keep it so hidden that no one can ever get to it and they complain the rest of their lives about that. Well, Leeland was pressing mine today.

"You really are a piece of shit," he said and smiled at me.

"Thanks," I said. "I think the same of you." I had no idea what he was saying. He had that way of talking to me, and I liked it. He got up and then lowered his cock, which was swollen and very fat, in front of me; aimed it right at me. "If I can't have your dick, you're going to have mine," he said. I wasn't going to fight that. His foreskin was heavy, with a lot of overhang. The head of his dick rarely poked through. Sometimes he'd skin the overflap back, and sometimes not. This time he didn't.

He squatted down and fed it to me, into my face. My tongue went out to his foreskin, then my mouth took in a good part of the first four or five inches of his meat. Soon I relaxed my throat, and he pushed his plug all the way down. I loved the way it filled my mouth up and I wanted to get it so far down into my throat that I could run my lips up his balls while he was down in me. He started fucking my face, and then grabbed my dick and started playing with it. He licked his hands slowly and rubbed the smouldering head of my dick against the spit in his palms.

He mouth-fucked me until I started gagging. I realized I might choke from his dick, which was now a lot thicker and fatter, but I couldn't stop either him or myself. I managed to take some air in. My eyes started tearing, and he pulled out for a moment, dragging with his cock a whole column of air, as if he was pulling it right out of my stomach. His meat had swollen a good bit, and the veins stood thick on it, like the veins on a man's arm after a workout.

"Dark mouth," he said. "Dark mouth. My dark mouth."

I nodded my head. "I want the rest," I told him. He told me not to worry. I'd get it. He stood up for a second and then shook his dick over me. I was still lying on the floor of the cubicle. I wondered what he was doing, till I felt a warm stream of piss on my sweaty stomach.

"You shitass," I said. I didn't want to be pissed on. I was not into piss. Then he put his large, rough foot on my chest and started to rub the piss into me with the palm of his heel. Suddenly, like the electricity was turned back on, I got turned on again, and started to take his foot into my mouth.

I was working over his foot, then I looked up. He had pinched off the tip of his foreskin. It was filling up with piss like a balloon. It started to look transparent, and I could see a network of purple and silver veins through it. It made his dick look tremendous, and transformed him in my mind into another, alien animal presence. I lost control of myself. I pulled him down to my mouth level and started to gobble his whole cock into my mouth. He dumped about a pint of hot piss down my throat and I continued sucking him, so that he kept his hard-on. He fucked me in the head some more, and I met each of his strokes, while he began to beat my meat. A few strokes later, he shot his thick egg-juice down me. I sucked it, swirling it around my mouth, down into my throat, and deeper into me. I came at the same time, exploding all over the floor of the room.

It took me a while to regain any form of balance. I felt like I'd been swimming out to sea with Leeland, and we finally hit land. Leeland got up and lay on the bed, and then lit one of my cigarettes. There were a lot of things I wanted to say to him, but I felt funny about saying any of them. I felt like I'd just been on a journey through several large but unexplored rooms in my own house: rooms I'd never gone into before. I hadn't let go like that in a long time; perhaps ever. While I knew that Leeland could tell just how much he turned me on, I thought to myself: Jesus, if I fell in love with this guy, it would be different. It would be, in fact, too difficult for me to deal with. It scared the hell out of me. But I knew this wasn't love; this was something I couldn't even name. The only thing I could say was that ... it was different.

"I'm going to have to go," he said. I tried to smile.

"A week from Wednesday?" I asked.

"No," he said. He closed his eyes. "I'm afraid I'm not going to get to see you anymore. My company is transferring me to the Midwest. Indiana. Can you believe? What rotten shit luck. It'll make the kids happy though. We told them they'll get a big house with a great big yard now."

I swallowed for a second. I realized I should look at him, because I wouldn't get to see him again. I looked at his eyes, that I could barely see in the dim light; his craggy face. "Good luck," I said.

He smiled and then knelt down next to me. He put his big hand through my hair. "Goodbye," he whispered. "Goodbye, dark mouth."

OHIO

K

Laramie used to tell me about his first sex sessions in Ohio, and I enjoyed hearing about them. Laramie was the sort of friend that I wanted to have when I left New York—that is, he was a hunk, but you might think he was just a brainless cowboy. He was by no way brainless, but sometimes you'd think he was. I don't know what it is about men like me and brainless cowboys—but the attraction is there. As Thelma Ritter said to Marilyn Monroe in Marilyn's last movie (okay, all you Marilyn fans—Marilyn's last *completed* movie) "The Misfits": "Cowboys are the last real men left on Earth." Now I know that today, when the Harvard MBA is supposed to convey Manhood, being the last real man is not that big of a deal. After all, the important question is: Does the last real man drive a Mercedes? But I have to admit, cowboys like Laramie turn me on, and I was happy as hell to meet him and talk to him—really talk—when I got the chance.

Laramie came from North Dakota, but his first Ohio friend was named 85 Blue. We were sitting in a very ratty diner that had some vile repute for a gay cliental, when Laramie whispered to me. "He had blue eyes. Blue like the sky. But sometimes I think they called him Blue because he blew men. What do you think of that?"

I pretended to be mighty shocked. To think that things like that went on in Ohio, close to Kentucky. Yes, even in Ohio. I let Laramie go on with his tale, while we walked back to his truck, and I noticed the funny way he walked, bowlegged in almost skintight jeans, like he'd been recently fucked by a horse, which I'm told is a cowboy characteristic. Laramie was getting up there a bit, and already had silvery whiskers on his face. He had sun lines around his eyes, and smoked Camels, unfiltered, which turned me on. He got into the truck, and his story, very much a confession to me, began.

"Blue," he said, as he backed the truck up, "had a long, hard body and the kind of cock that went with it. Great dong. Uncut. I saw it the first time when he passed me buck naked on the way to the shower. But Blue was the kind of guy who was so natural and so sweet that naturally, you'd want to play with him. Know what I mean?"

I told him I did. And then Laramie went on with the rest of this story, which is his, and I'll let him tell it:

Blue had a long hard body and a cock that naturally went with it. It looked kind of silvery at night, I remember that from a lot of nights staying up with him. He was the first guy I ever made it with, and once I started, I couldn't keep my hands off him. Sometimes I'd put a little spit on his tool, and then juice it up until the big head, all pink and sweet and kind of rosy looking, started to work its way out.

"Wha'cha do that for?" Blue'd always ask, and wink.

"You like it?"

"Sure do," Blue would say, when we got in the back, behind the tool shed of Uncle Willy's farm where I worked with him. We usually went back there to hose off, but ended up fiddling with each other. One thing, you know, leading to another. At the end of a hot day, it was fun to take your pants down and start fiddling with your pecker out there, just behind the big field. There was nothing to look in on you, but that big Ohio sun.

That first evening when it happened, Blue and I were so tired from chores out in the fields, fixing fences and stuff like that, that we ended up back there. The place was owned by Willy, who'd been in Ohio for years. My own family's from North Dakota, but Willy was Ohio-born, and he stayed there and had a nice place. When I close my eyes, I can still smell Willy's farm and that tool shed in back. Heavy motor oil from the tractors. Dry wheat in the distant fields. Animals. Some horses, sheep, rabbits, chickens. Willy had an all-around farm. Something you don't see much anymore. And that first summer away from North Dakota, it was a nice place to work.

That evening, Blue was quick to strip off his overalls. He never wore underwear. Patterns of sunburn made streaks on his white skin where he'd open the side flaps in the fields to let the wind cool his ass. He had very blond Ohio skin. I guess part German. Everybody in North Dakota seems to be dark from Irish or Indian blood, but Blue was blond. His skin was fine, and thin so you could see veins through it, but he had a lot of blond hair on his chest. There was a spigot with a nylon hose in the tool shed. I dragged the hose around to the back of the shed, and there was nothing but Willy's fields behind us.

"Sure nobody can see us?" Blue asked.

I told him sure. "You wanted to get wet, didn't you?" I fumbled with the nozzle of the nylon hose and blasted Blue, who was stark naked now, with the water turned up as high as it would go. I aimed it at his big white chest. He had little titties that looked like pink strawberries. They were smooth and sort of flat, but they raised easily when Blue got excited. I'm sure he was excited then, because the water was cold. It was so cold that it must have felt hot at first.

Blue screamed. "Stop that!" but I only aimed the hose lower, down to Blue's belly. His stomach was hard and streaked with salt-sweat in the furrows where he sat on the tractor.

Then Blue started laughing. I guess he got used to the cold and it must have felt great after the heat that afternoon. "Lower," he called to me. "Get that damn hose lower!"

I complied. I aimed the hose lower, until it just tickled his big, low-hanging balls. The cold water from the hose made his balls pull up and get smaller, while his pecker got bigger—and harder, too. I watched while his peter's rosy head started to slide out.

"You know what?" I said to Laramie.

"What, Fuckhead?" Blue said. Fuckhead was one of Blue's pet words. He used it while we were out in the fields. He said he had a horse he used to call Fuckhead, too. So it was kind of a family name. "What, Fuckhead?"

"You know what your peter looks like?"

"Naw—tell me." He cupped his nuts in his thick hands and aimed his cock, now hard, directly at me. "I bet you think it looks just like a gun, don't you, Fuckhead?"

I told him I was just going to say that, and I'm sure I must have blushed. I was only about twenty at this time. I never had as much experience with sex as I wanted people to believe. I was no virgin, but I still blushed. I was tanned, and I must have blushed right under my tan.

Blue only laughed. He put his hands on my bare shoulders. "Why don'cha take off your jeans, and then I can squirt you. Or are you scared of your own medicine?"

"I'm not scared," I said, then added: "I wear underwear."

Blue smirked. "I won't hold it against you."

I started to unzip my jeans. They were really new, straight from Montgomery Ward. Still dark and tight, especially around the crotch and legs. It was a chore to get them down. They wouldn't slide off that easily. "What's wrong?" Blue asked. "Is your little pecker hard already." So what if it was? I admitted. "I'm not ashamed. You get yours hard and it doesn't bother me."

Blue nodded his head. He smiled at me. "This ain't like North Dakota, ain't it? You miss it out there?"

I told him I did. I was determined to see a lot of the world that summer. After I left Uncle Willy's, I was going to take a train up to Canada, and see some really big mountains, and maybe stay the winter in Alberta, where my Mom had cousins.

"I bet you just got a little pecker," Blue jested with me. He was always getting on to me how young I was. I had no hair on my chest. It's probably from Indian blood. Indians have no chest hair at all. I was a fresh-faced kid, and I knew it.

"It's not small at all!" I protested.

"Little teeny weeny!" Blue said. "Big as a squirrel's!"

"Shit! Shut up!" I said. "It's gonna come out as soon as I get these damn new jeans down."

Then I saw Blue watch me real close, while I still tried to get my jeans down. Finally, they were down, and I stood in front of him in my white Jockey shorts. Suddenly, I wasn't sure I wanted them off. Blue'd never seen me buck naked before—but I'd seen him. He squinted his eyes, like he was watching every movement I made. I felt self-conscious—like what the hell was going on? So, my dick was circumcised and his wasn't. What was so bad about that? And I was younger by a few years, although I felt a lot younger. I'd hardly been away from North Dakota. The air got very quiet and hot.

"You ain't gonna take those off?" he asked me.

"I'm not sure," I said. "I'm tired of you making fun of me."

The smile dropped off Blue's face. "Would you mind, young man," he said seriously to me, "if I hold that hose you got in your hand? If you want to just leave, I can squirt myself."

I twisted the nozzle shut, and then quietly handed it to Blue. I was about to go back to the front of the shed to wrestle my jeans back on, when Blue twisted the nozzle back into business and squirted the hell out of me from the rear. He got my jeans, that were off on the ground, soaking, too.

88

"What-the-FUCK-didja-do-that-for?" I shouted. I turned to him. I was furious. I did not go in for playing around like that. I was so angry, I was about to hit him, when he squirted me again, straight in the face, full blast. I had to keep my eyes closed, to keep the water out, and while I did that, I felt his hands drag down my Jockeys, and his mouth suddenly hit my cock.

I thought I was going to fall apart right then. My knees started shaking while he went to work on my dick. He was kneeling in a puddle of mud and motor oil, and kissing my balls and getting a full head of wang in his mouth all at once, so it seemed. I didn't know what to do, so all I did was press his face into my crotch, and I enjoyed it.

He got up. "Surprised?" he said, and kissed me on my mouth. "You're a real treasure," he said. "I like your dick. I thought for a moment that you were never gonna get those jeans off."

I looked into Blue's eyes. They reflected the warm sky of the fields beyond the back of the shed. I wasn't sure what to do next. I'd heard about guys who did this sort of thing to you. My daddy had warned me once about "strange dudes," but I never thought any of them would be like Blue. Suddenly, I just grabbed hold of his pale chest, with all that blond hair on it, and he grabbed one of my hands and led it to his cock. "I guess you'd like to play with this," he said to me.

I wasn't sure what to do, I told him.

"Don'chu worry none about that," he told me. "I'll show you."

I started playing with his cock in my hand. It was a whole new experience for me. When I was a kid, we had jack-off sessions with other boys, but we never touched each other. You were never supposed to do that. I'd once thought about it, and now there I was doing it.

Blue's body started to quiver as his pony—that was an old name we kids in North Dakota used to have for dicks—got harder. I could tell his pony was getting really ready to ride. He held on to me, and suddenly slid back down and started sucking me again. He really knew how to do it; that was for sure. A girl I knew once did it to me, but she was a rank amateur compared to Blue as he slid down into the oily wet dirt behind the tool shed. Everything was getting down to the real nitty gritty. I can tell you that. The water from the hose made the ground wet as oatmeal, and some dirt ran up the blond crack of Blue's ass, but his hot mouth wouldn't stop. My cock felt sweet and silky in his mouth, while his tongue licked at my cock head.

"I bet you just love to do that," I said. This was all new and nice to me. It reminded me of the first time I ever got on a motorcycle. At first I was kind of scared of it, then I really liked it.

Blue stopped for a second. He got up. His thighs and legs were covered with oily dirty water. It made his lower body glisten, and his upper body look that much whiter. "You like gittin' your cock done, don'cha, baby?"

"Sure," I said. "I guess you wanna take my load?"

"You ready now to pop?"

I nodded that I was. I was really ready for just about anything by that time. Blue was some cowboy, I discovered, and he certainly knew what to do with my pony. The sky was getting much darker. Suddenly, I wondered about my uncle. I figured he was at home, sitting his fat ass down in front of the big TV set in his den. His house was a big one, with wall-to-wall Orlon carpet, and it was just around the bend. What a surprise he'd get if he just happened to decide to cut off the TV and go driving down near his barn.

"Sure, I'm ready," I told Blue.

Blue got down again, and started chomping at my meat, really sucking it, and this time, I put my legs around his neck. Blue grabbed my ass, and started slapping me lightly as he sucked me. I was hard as an ice cube, and hot! Real hot. Ice hot! It didn't take long for Blue to get me off, and later Blue told me that my jism was as sweet as butter off an ear of corn.

I had to catch my breath for a second. There are certain things you never, ever forget, and your first real great blow job from a man is one of them. I looked at Blue—he was still hard and ready and I knew that he wanted something. But I wasn't sure what. He approached me, and gently turned me over, right there in that oily dirt behind the tool shed. But it was real dark now. He put some of his spit into my asshole, and I just relaxed and let him in. It felt nice with Blue's big, uncut prong in my hole. He stayed in there, very gentle like. This was something nobody every told me about— believe me, no girl had ever done this to me before! He didn't pound at me at all. He just gently rode me, and he was so hot that it didn't take Blue more than a few minutes to get his pony home.

"That was so nice," Blue said to me, while we were both naked, and lying on our backs in the dirt. By this time, we were too squishy and wet to care. "You're one nice boy. I never thought old Willy Johnson would have such a nice nephew!"

I thanked him. We hosed each other off, and dried off as best we could with some paper towels from the tool shed. My jeans were still wet, but they seemed easier to get into now—I guess they must have stretched some. Then we got into Blue's old Dodge, and rode over to Uncle Willy's house. Like I expected, he was stretched out in front of the TV in that tacky den of his. I stayed on the front porch, while Blue went in for his paycheck—Willy owed him some back pay. When Blue came back with a smile on his face, we got back into the Dodge and headed into town, this tiny place called Whitley that was just a few filling stations, a grocery store, and a Western Auto. There was a diner in town, and Blue treated me to dinner.

Then we went to a drive-in movie a few miles out of town. They still had drive-ins in that part of Ohio, and I was glad, because even though the movie—something about Teenage Werewolves from Outer Space—wasn't that great, I did something I'd never done before. I gave a man a blow job in the front seat of a Dodge. That certainly made going to the drive-in a different experience to me from then on. When we left the drive-in, Blue asked me how I liked the movie, and I told him, "Well, I never saw anything like that in North Dakota!"

THE TRICK WHO FELL FROM SPACE

I know—I mean I *know*—you won't believe this story about my friend Gary. That is, I call him Gary. But I've got to tell it to somebody. I'm not even sure why I should tell it to you, but sometimes you keep things a secret for too long and you even start to believe that nothing's real, and before long, you're screwy, and you're ready to be sent away, if you know what I mean.

Maybe I should tell you how I found out about Gary, but I know what I'll do, I'll tell you *how* I found him. That's the best way to begin. I'll tell you just how I found him.

Okay, you're not going to believe this. Shit! You're going to think I'm crazy, but alright, I'm going to tell you the whole thing anyway. He was stark naked. Gorgeous and *stark* naked. That's the first thing I've got to tell you.

I was living in Atlanta—actually right outside of Atlanta, in this wonderful little town called Dawsonville. It was pretty and quiet, and the people were very polite. But it was a strange place to live. If you get my drift. That is, I was sure I was the only ho-mo-sexual there. (People in this part of the world always say the word like they've never heard it before. As in, "Is he a ho-MO-sexual?" They figure if they put enough "Mo" in it, we'll all go

91

away.)

To be truthful with you, I'm sure there were others, because when I'd go out cruising in my car, which is the only way to go cruising in the Atlanta area, I'd usually find somebody in about ten miles. Usually, he'd be messing around in some park or at some rest stop. Often he'd be married, one way or another, and just out "for a little air," from the kids, wife, or his own husband. Although the rest stops get their occasional shake-up from the various cops, who must get bonuses from busting cocksucking thieves in the bushes (you never can tell when they're going to steal a bench or a picnic basket or do something else abominable like that), the rest stops along the interstates are busy locations in my neck of the woods. In fact, you can make a whole gay career out of rest stops in the Greater Atlanta area. Let me tell you that, personally.

Well, that day, a while back—it was October and still very warm—I was, as they say, "tooling" out on the highway and I knew that at the junction of Highways 23 and 129, where the state road hits a decent-sized country road, there was a real hot rest stop. I was as horny as a wide-mouthed bass in heat, and all I really wanted to do was strip off all of my clothes and cavort in the woods a bit and suck some dick. I know, you think I'm a terrible person without an inch of socially redeeming value, but haven't we all felt like that sometimes?

So, I got to the stop and damn, it was full of kids and families. They were yammering and blabbering at the two picnic tables, which were all set out with baskets of KFC chicken and those type of salads that begin with Kraft Miracle Whip and end up with canned fruit cocktail and little pieces of marshmallow in them. I was immediately disappointed, but I noticed that there were more than just two cars parked in the lot, so I used my amazing powers of deduction to figure that something or other had to be going on farther up the creek at the end of a little-used path, up a steep hill just above the small picnic area where the families were beginning to divvy up the drumsticks from the white meat.

So I put my wallet in the glove compartment of my Datson, locked it, then locked the car and left. I always carried a few dollars and some change, my plastic pouches of K-Y, just in case I got real lucky, and some pre-lubed rubbers, which are wonderful because they're so portable. I mean, if you plan ahead and have any sense, you can carry a whole sex kit in one front pocket of a snap shirt.

So, after briefly waving to all the tiny tykes down below, I started climbing up the path. It was a gorgeous day. I mean *gorrr-juss!* The sky was so blue you could have seen your face in it, and the trees were shiny with leaves—nothing had changed colors yet. The climb up the hill, above the picnic area, was kind of steep, but my heart was really pounding from

92

expectation and excitement, not just exertion. I mean, I was so horny that if I didn't find anything, I was going to jerk off anyway and watch my wad glisten in the grass or a bush or just do anything crazy like that. I love being naked outside and sometimes that's such a turn-on to me that even just feeling my butt and nuts brush against leaves or soft, high grass without a pair of chinos or Levis between them and the world gets me going.

I couldn't wait to get my clothes off. Like I said, I was real horny and I was also, let me tell you, a bit anxious. I mean, let's face it, I figured I'd better darn keep my ear to the ground, like the Scouts do, just in case one of those families decided to start nature hiking. I could see them calling the State Police, and as we all know, things out in the rolling hills of rural Georgia are not *quite* as sweet and simple as we'd all like them to be all the fucking time.

Anyway, when I rounded the bend at the tail end of the path, in some pretty high grass, with all this beautiful mountain laurel around—Jesus, they are so pretty—I started to strip my clothes off. First, I snapped open my shirt, and then took it off. My nibs—you know, *tits*—they just loved it. My body was tanned and the slight cool of the air made them start to harden like little jelly beans and the hairs on my stomach, which were bleached kind of copper, started to rake off in the wind a bit, just ripple on my chest. Shit, it all felt *goooood*.

I felt so damn good that I decided to take everything off and I peeled down to my sneakers and socks. I would have taken them off, too, but you know there is such a thing as poison ivy in this part of Georgia, and I did need to watch out for it. But I'm sure that the grass itself wouldn't have hurt my bare feet.

I'd been wearing a comfortable old jockstrap. I love wearing jocks, but I took that off as well. I figured why not go buck-ass natural? It was such a beautiful, natural place and every part of me started to come alive, right then. That's why I like to live out in the country. There are a lot of hick country people I can live without, the kind who think the KKK is a social service organization. They can be the fly in the ointment of rural living. But just the thrill of being out there, with my whole body starting to suck in that fresh air—okay, you can sure tell I was getting into it all—when "just around the corner," or about twenty feet from where I shucked off my jock, I saw this figure coming out of the creek. I thought my heart was going to collapse. I couldn't make out all the details, but what I did see was wonderful, I mean—Gosh!—what a strapping man! *All there!* I mean, he was naked as a fucking mud beaver, and he was right there in front of me. All I had to do was walk over to him.

You know, sometimes you have this feeling that a twenty dollar bill has been dropped by God's ever loving hand right there in front of you—well, in a way, that was what this was. I just smiled and walked straight over to him. I can still remember the way the grass crunched under my sneakers. My heart was beating so hard that my ears started to tingle. I'll never forget it. I kept trying to keep my hard-on from getting too hard. I know that the head of my thick little pecker must have been purple by then, but I kept trying to keep it from standing out at full mast as I got closer to this man-thing.

He had just got out of the creek, and was sitting down in a very sunny spot, drying himself naturally. He was about six-foot tall, and he was—I know you're not going to believe this—perfectly built. It was like he came right off the hunk machine itself. He was a *hunkeroo*! His shoulders and his chest were perfect, broad, I mean deep where they were supposed to be. He had everything. I mean I couldn't see all the details, but I expected that the cock that went with all of the above would not disappoint me, either.

He was bronzy colored, from a whole summer out of doors, I was sure. And he had deep, thick chestnut hair, so deep it was almost mahogany in places.

Suddenly, he turned around to me when I approached, and he just looked at me. And he smiled. I mean it was the most wonderful, open-mouthed smile I have ever seen since I was about eight years old, when kids really smiled at you and hadn't learned to be frightened of smiling yet. I mean, here we were, smiling at each other, and naked as jaybirds in this beautiful setting.

My mouth just dropped open. I didn't say anything for—shit, it must have been about a full minute—and he just looked at me, and he didn't say anything, either. But I kept looking at him, at his gorgeous chest, with just that slight amount of dark, almost mahogany hair on it. His chest tapered down to a perfect triangle and met with his waist. Not an inch of fat on him; it was such a natural waist, the kind you want to put your hands on. Then he got up and I could tell—*immediately*—that that throbbing, big-man-cock of his was just as *happy* to see my dick as my peter was to see him.

"Hi," I finally said, and he grinned at me and, then—God, did I dream all this?—he opened up his arms. It was like we had stopped thinking, worrying, getting aggravated and bothered, and just did what we wanted to do. The next few seconds spun by. I wanted to say some kind of bullshit, but I'm proud to say I didn't. All he did was just hold me, and then his large mouth opened and he kissed me. He had soft, warm lips and a clean, milky kind of breath, and I felt his lips glide over my face, right onto my mouth and then his thick, strong tongue settled into my mouth and filled it. My eyes closed. I could have creamed right then.

We started to roll around, buck naked, in the grass. I was sure some sort of snake was going to bite me and, hell, I wouldn't even know it! My hands kept roaming and touching him on his chest and that wonderful place where a man's hips melt into his ass, and then his butt which was as firm and warm as I ever wanted a man-butt to be.

Well, I just let go. I mean, I became one rip-roaring, hells-a-poppin', hundred perfect horny-ass faggot! My mouth couldn't get enough of him into it. I started at his nibs, which were wonderful, like hard little boners themselves, and went right down his chest, into his navel and then down to that place I told you about, just right there where the hips and the ass met—where some people, like *most* of us, have love handles—and I just chewed on that spot for a few seconds. Then I got his dick in my hands. I started to suck it. I mean, first I licked it, then just—shit!—put the whole dang thing into my mouth, from the thick, gorgeous head down to the veins almost at the very base, by his balls. Wow! What a trip that was—landed the whole airplane all the way—and he let go this deep, sweet "Ahhhh," as if he loved every, scrumptious second of it.

And he was so responsive. Sometimes you meet guys and they're like wood. Nice statues to look at, but they're so tight and wooden you think you're going to get splinters from their dicks. This one was not. He kept twisting himself around to kiss me. He just wanted to kiss and kiss and kiss, and his hands were groping me and pulling at my dick-pipe, and I had to hold my pipe back, just to prolong it, 'cause my nuts were turning blue, they wanted to blast so much.

Then we finally got ourselves around into the most wonderful sixty-nine in all of God's creation, let me tell you. I was just stuffing his meat, all half a foot or so of it into my mouth, and feeling my tongue work on it, when I realized something.

It was a strange thing to realize. He had a third ball. I kid you not. This creature, nameless unto me, had *three* balls. At some point in my meanderings about his fabulous genitals with my intrepid tongue, I felt three balls.

Now, I have gone down on men with *one* ball. That is an unfortunate, but not uncommon situation. But *three* balls, and I realized that this was not your average run-of-the-mill trick. No wonder this guy was so oversexed.

Well, I thought, this *is* a fucking miracle. I mean, of all the humans in the world, I, George, should get a fucking three-balled man. So, I just decided, why complain when you stumble on the gold fields? And I started to take all three of them, one by one, into my hot mouth and caress them in his ball-sack. And he was happy. Boy, was he happy. And I was happy, too. And, boy, was I ready to come my brains out.

But I held back a couple of minutes more, and he did, too. Until I just managed to get his cock out of my mouth—the head was so pretty then—and I said, "Man, I'm going to do it," and he didn't say anything, but a second later, he shot his wad into my mouth, and I took my dick out of him and blasted my cum all over his face. I'm not sure why that happened. It just did.

It took me a couple of minutes to return to Earth—full consciousness, so to speak—and I held on to him. I'm not sure which part I held on to, but it was some part between his wonderful, firm belly and his sweet ass. Then I realized where I was, and what I'd been doing, and I was really happy.

I looked over at him. I smiled and he smiled back. Then I did what I always do. Maybe it's a reflex, but it seemed like the most natural thing to ask. "What's your name?" I said.

He smiled. It took him a second, then he said, "Gary."

I smiled again. I liked looking at him. "Mine's George. Boy, that was wonderful!"

He got up and took my hand. My body was still itching from excitement and Georgia grass flies, and we went over to the creek. It felt great—cool but not icy—just great. We started to hold each other and I sucked on his nibs some more, and then I started to notice something else about him. Right above his ass, just at that point where normally the tailbone ends—a point that I really love to feel on a man—he had a small, very hairy projection. I wouldn't want to call this a tail, but it was certainly about as close to one as I ever felt on a human person.

But why point out peculiarities? I was happy. I couldn't help beaming. I love to smile, and I did. I felt goony with happiness. I lightly bit his ear lobe and then whispered into his ear, "You're a strange guy."

"Uh huh," he whispered back. Then he smiled, and he laughed. It was a dry, intelligent laugh, I will say, and I started to laugh with him. Then I started to feel him up some more. I had my hands around his peter, and I remembered his third ball.

I kissed him. My mouth just opened up around his. Then I said, in a whisper, "I've never made it with a guy who had three nuts before."

We got out of the creek. The water was starting to feel cold by then, and the air was so much warmer. I gathered up my clothes. We lay in the sun for a while, and then I put my jock on and he was still naked.

"Where are your clothes?" I asked him. I'd lit a cigarette. I don't smoke much, but after sex there's still nothing like one.

He looked at me and grinned. "I don't have any."

"You what?"

He shrugged his large, beautiful shoulders. "I don't have any. At least, I don't remember where I put them." He smiled sheepishly. "It's just a blank."

I nodded my head, like I actually understood what he was saying. "Where are you from?" I asked. He was lying on top of my left biceps, in the tall grass and we were looking straight up, into the sky, which had become slightly darker. It was about four o' clock and getting cooler now.

"I'm from a long way from here. A *long* way, George. Do you think we can go back with you, to your house?"

"But you don't have any clothes," I said.

"Don't worry. There won't be any people. I can tell you that already."

I was puzzled. Very puzzled. But this was not something I could just walk away from. We got up. I put on my clothes, and walked with him—he still naked—through the tall grasses, and around the bend, until we got to the parking. I was frightened. You never can tell when some Georgia state trooper, who might not look so kindly upon these things, might decide to pop up. But, just like he said, there was nobody there. He walked like being barefoot was very natural to him. The gravel in the parking lot didn't bother him. He showed me his car. It was an old, old one. I think it was a Studebaker, that's how old it was, with a Utah license plate.

"You actually drove that?"

He nodded his head, and he got into my car. Luckily, I had a tee shirt and an old pair of cut-offs in the back. I would've been happy as a pig in shit just to drive while he was naked, but truthfully, I don't live in the most sophisticated part of Dawsonville, and I could just imagine some of the hicks in my neighborhood when I drove up and naked *hunkerama* got out.

In October, the sun, although warm enough, goes down faster, and it was twilight when we got home. My dog, Scooter, greeted us loudly at the door to my one-bedroom "condo" which I rent. It's called a "condo" because the real estate people think that's the hot thing for single people to live in. It's a "Condo Community" out there in the middle of the fucking sticks, which means that it also has a Jacuzzi hot tub in the back, which I have enjoyed on many a hot night, with many a trick, and a swimming pool, which is for the birds—too full of "singles" and too chlorinated.

I was hungry, so I pulled out some ice cream and some stuff like bananas and strawberries and I wanted to slather it and stuff it up various parts of Gary, but held myself back. I put the ice cream and fruit and stuff into two bowls, and we ate it on the carpet in the living room. Scooter, a fuzzy, brown part-terrier—part whatever, watched us a for while, then went under the sofa. He has this real ability to know when I'm not in the mood to pet him and want to pet somebody else. I'd eat some of the vanilla ice cream, then sucked on Gary's cock while my mouth was still cold. We got each other too hot for comfort and ended up in the bedroom. He'd never seen one of my rubbers, and of course I was too happy to show him how to use it. After I'd stretched one over his thick meat, I went down on it, a special treat, I must say, for the safe sex generation.

"Are you scared of AIDS?" he asked me.

I just smiled. I didn't want to think about that then. He fucked me so nice and afterwards we took the rubber off and I swear I wanted to suck it out, but I was afraid I was getting a little gross.

We lay on the bed for a while. I wasn't sure what I was going to do then. Then he said to me, "I don't have the same immune system you do."

"You what?"

"Where I come from, we already had the AIDS problem. We got rid of it. So my immune system is different."

I kissed him again. "A lot about you is different. Tell me about yourself. I want to know."

"I'm a real foreigner," he began. He held me very closely and was really whispering. "It would take you five years to get where I come from. But human beings have never gone that fast."

Suddenly it dawned on me that he was saying something I really couldn't understand. So I asked him the first question that came into my mind. "How come you're a homosexual?"

"We have three sexes there. I'm just one of them. It's very normal there to be what you call 'homosexual.'"

"It is?"

He nodded his head.

"You mean no one arrests you there for it, or bothers you, or hassles you ever?"

"No."

"It must be a nice place."

He turned his head away from me. "It's dying," he said. "One of our anti-pollutant systems backfired. The entire habitable part of the planet had to be evacuated. Everybody I knew went to our moon, but I ended up here."

"Here in Dawsonville?"

"No, in Utah."

That made sense; the license plate and all. Utah was big, open, and lots of it was fairly empty. I looked at him much closer. God, his body was so beautiful and it had this wonderful warmth to it. I also noticed that he had six toes on each foot, a remnant of a tail, and three balls. Aside from that, he could pass as one of us, probably better than I could.

"Would you let me stay with you for a while?" he asked. "Money will not be a problem. My mental powers are good at getting around money—remember that I knew there was no one waiting for us at the parked cars? I can use those powers at machines that involve computers. But I must be careful that my transactions are not suspect and traced—so I cannot be greedy. I have some money in my car. I have used these powers to speak your language. But I have not been able to get any clothes, and have not met many people here."

He said all this calmly, as if everything he did was ordinary. He was right about the clothes—he didn't have a stitch of them. How he ever got all the way from Utah naked was more of a mystery to me than how he found me at the rest stop. I found out there were many strange things I'd learn to expect from Gary. His amazing intelligence, which seemed to float over things and then catch them, was only one of them.

He was very foreign. He stayed with me for a week. I'm not sure if part of the turn-on of this guy was that I couldn't tell anyone what he was really about, where he'd come from, or the secrets of his delicious body. But he was a complete turn-on anyway. He seemed to understand everything I ever wanted from sex, and with three balls, he was insatiable. We must have fucked in 62 different positions, and Scooter got used to staying under the couch, because we did it on every square inch of the living room, the bedroom, the bathroom, and even the kitchen.

He left as mysteriously as the way he came into my life. I just know that one day there was no old car with Utah plates parked next to my space in the "Condo" lot. But I keep hoping that one day he'll call or write, or maybe I'll be at another rest stop and find him.

He liked Atlanta. He said that it reminded him of the place he'd come from. Everything was either underground or air conditioned; there were parts of town you didn't walk into; there were dangers from people you considered alien. He made me realize how science fiction the South had become. It really opened my eyes up about a lot of things. We went to several malls and bought clothes. I remember him saying, "Why do they put a roof over the sky? Why don't they just let the sky in?" I nodded my head and tried to see the world through his eyes. And for the first time in a long time, from that summer day, maybe when I was twelve years old, and had my first hard-on when I saw a hunky naked man next to me in the showers of the downtown Lucky Street YMCA, I felt less foreign than the person next to me.

THE VOICE WITHIN THE IDOL

Many years ago, when I was a young man about New York, I had the good fortune, or misfortune—depending upon your point of view—of getting too drunk one night and being left by my friends at the home of my host. It had been a wild party, in a beautiful section of Manhattan where it seemed like the very night air was sprayed with a particularly suffocating form of cologne you'd find in Bloomingdale's, but I still had no intentions of spending the night. My host, a man at least twenty years older than me, had been quite successful in business. His apartment was showy; his hospitality, especially to young men, lavish. In other words, he lived in some splendor for a guy who'd never seen the inside of a college, had never had much talent for doing anything except pleasing the right people, and who still spoke like a resident of the less frequented side of the tracks.

Like I said, after passing out cold in his living room, I had the excellent fortune of ending up in his bedroom. Now, although I was young, I still thought that these almost Arabian Nights maneuvers, when suddenly one finds oneself transported—as if by a genie—from one location, in this instance the living room, to another, the bedroom, boded for good luck. And I was right. My host turned out to be as pleasing in the sack, in this case a huge bed with satin sheets and a mirror on the ceiling, as he'd been during the earlier part of the evening, when my foolish young friends deserted me for what they felt to be the greener pastures of the bars and discos of a wintry night. Although the hair on my host's head resembled the gray of ashes, the fire in his loins was still very red hot. And after finding myself stirred in the early dawn hours by his passionate kisses, I soon also found myself quite awake and very hard. It is these surprises which add luster to the routine of our lives, and which my other young friends had dismissed by quickly leaving for the relative boredom of another night out. But by the circumstance of my drunkenness, I discovered a side to our host that my friends denied themselves.

That next morning, over an elaborate breakfast served on Limoges and chocolated coffee laced with an expensive liqueur, my host told me he would reward my decision to spend the night—unplanned as it was—with a story that had been told to him under remarkably similar circumstances, perhaps twenty-five years earlier. I told him that there was no need to reward me at all. But he demurred and said I should listen to his story first, before I made up my mind.

"I hope you'll never forget this story, young man," he added. "Because I certainly haven't."

I sat there, quite enchanted by the luxury of my setting, in a large, velvet robe, at the table in his formal dining room. I looked up curiously at him from my gilt-rimmed coffee cup, and asked him what the story was called.

He smiled benignly at me. "It is called, my dear young friend, 'The Voice Within the Idol.'"

In ancient Egypt, many years ago, there was once an idol. The idol stood in the recesses of a large, dark, stone temple at the edge of the great desert. The idol had been left by an army of invaders. They had brought the idol with them, and venerated it during their time of conquest. And although the idol was not native to Egypt, the natives in turn treated the foreign god with great respect, as he was known to be powerful, to reward all wishes, allay all fears, and bring happiness, serenity, and security if approached correctly.

Many, many people of every social stripe came to see the idol, and they all hoped to hear his voice. Physically, the idol was very striking, with a massive, sculpted chest; great, muscular thighs and legs; and a powerful, bull neck. But the most striking thing was his face. The face was quite featureless, with a smooth, bland countenance. In other words, one could read into the idol's expression pretty much what one wanted. To some, the idol was fearful and threatening; to others, kind and comforting; and to others, still, very seductive.

The idol's voice was famous. Some people had heard it and boasted thereafter of being given their heart's desire. But to hear the idol's voice, you had to come alone, under the darkness of a late, late night; or even later, just as the gracious morning star arose. The idol, as a rule, would not speak to groups. Since the way to the idol was so forbidding, out there at the edge of an inhospitable desert, and the idol himself *did* appear so frightening to a great number of people, few ever attempted a private audience with this large, stone enigma.

And, further, those who did were very circumspect about reporting the effects of the idol's voice. Certainly, the voice was deep, commanding, knowledgeable—even exciting. And those who came alone reported that they stood trembling in awe. They did exactly what the idol wished them to do, whether it was to bring offerings, or listen to the idol's gift of prophecy, or even to the idol's own petty wishes and regrets. Because, as everyone knew, sometimes you had to do that with idols. But those who did venture alone up to the temple at the edge of the desert, in the deepest, most frightening hour of night, said very little else.

One evening a young man, first making his way through this treacherous world, decided that he, too, had to see the idol. And he had to see him alone. He had gone to the idol several times in groups with his friends. They were a chatty group—young students of the Mysteries, of the Arts, or Commerce; and they'd all been awed by the idol. What massive proportions the idol displayed! What huge hands! What huge feet! Even his large male member—how they exclaimed about his large male member! Wasn't it supposed to have magical powers of its own? But in groups, no one ever heard the idol's voice. The idol was silent; silent as the centuries he came from. Finally, the young man decided that it was high time that he heard the idol's voice for himself.

"Be careful," his friends warned. "The desert at night is terrifying. Jackals. Wild beasts. Shrieking ghosts. They all prowl the desert at night and come up to the very edge where the idol's temple sits. Many men have been known never, ever, to come back."

These were daunting warnings, and for a moment the young man was discouraged. But he was a cocky young fellow, who as a rule did not listen to his chatty friends, and his sense of adventure and ambition quickly got the most of him. He jumped on his horse and galloped past the palms and the last settlements lit with torches, to the place where the invaders had built their temple. There the only light came from a thin moon and the desert stars.

He steeled his courage up, and walked through the huge, long, dark entranceway. Scorpions brushed from his path. Small wild cats screeched. Rats and snakes hurried away. Bats swooshed over his head. His heart drummed inside his young, handsome chest. The way, in almost total darkness, seemed to take forever. His eyes became more accustomed—then some pale light from the moon and the stars began to seep into the recesses of the temple.

Finally, many yards ahead, he saw the idol. It was huge. It was frightening. "Co-o-oome!" it said.

His knees went to water. He thought he'd collapse. The idol at night was as frightening as he'd ever heard. And that *voice!* It could move boulders. It could stop an army. It was the biggest, deepest, most thunderous voice the young man had ever heard.

He approached. To his sheer terror, he saw, in his nervousness, that the idol's face, normally so bland, was scowling. *The idol was displeased.* "Whaaaaat do you want?" the idol asked.

"Oh," the young man said, his voice pinched and tense. "Just to be happy." He paused a second. Although the palms of his hands were cold, he was perspiring. But he knew what he had to do, and he had to ask the idol what he had galloped through the wilderness to ask. "I want," he said, swallowing hard, "to know my way through life. To have *all* the answers. Not to fear anyone. I want that."

"Doo-oon't we all!!!" the idol said. His mouth appeared to turn down. "Go-ooo!!" the idol boomed.

The young man felt terrible. Dejected. He'd come so far, and now he'd been rejected by the idol. This was not the way it was supposed to end. He turned around and began to walk sadly off.

"No-ooo!!! Not home!" the idol roared. "Not *that* way! Go left."

The young man was shaken to his sandals at first, but then he collected himself and walked to the left. There, in an even deeper recess of the ancient temple, he saw a narrow passageway. He followed it. It was very dark and close and silent. He could hear his own breathing. He could hear his own heartbeat. A dozen steps away, the passageway ended abruptly. A blank wall hit him. There was no light at all. Nothing for him to do. No place for him to go. He felt ambushed. Up against a blank wall, at the end of a narrow passageway ...

Then he heard the idol's voice speak once more. "There! Stay!"

Well, where else was he going to go? There was no place else. It was too dark to see. The young man decided simply to stay and see what the old gods and their idol had in mind.

Suddenly, a hand reached for him. Was it the idol's hand? Would it put its hand around his young, innocent neck and kill him?

But the hand seemed amazingly gentle, and then there was another hand. Both hands held him around his waist. Then the hands bade him to lie down—flat on his stomach.

"Now!" the idol said in the darkness at the end of the passageway. "Now, you will get the answer."

The answer? the young man thought as he lay on his stomach. Finally, the answer! "What? What?" he asked.

"*This!*"

The young man felt something coming at him, under his light, Egyptian robes. Then he felt something enter his body, from his rear end. It was large. But it wasn't *that* large. Actually, to tell the truth, it was about as large as any normal man might be. Nothing big by idol standards, but no small potatoes, either. He'd heard about this ... this ... humiliation, this horror that happened to young men when they weren't careful and went abroad at night into the underbelly of the City or the Desert.

But, after about half a second, he realized that it didn't feel all that bad. And, actually, since he couldn't go any further in the temple, and it was pitch dark, *and* the idol was such a hunky, fearful, awful creature anyway ... well, that was just the end of that.

The idol quickly took his pleasure from the young man, and the young man had to admit that he'd felt worse things before. And, specifically speaking, it was rather exciting in fact. In fact, he couldn't believe anything so marvelous could happen to a simple young man like himself, alone at the edge of the desert.

After it was over—and the idol pulled himself out of the young man's anatomy—there was a moment of intense quiet. The young man had indeed never heard quiet this quiet. He was certain that he was alone in the recesses of the temple, and the great idol who'd just mounted him had left. Now, what was he to do? Now, he'd never know a single secret. He suppressed a sob. Now, he'd have to go back to his friends and lie to them, because certainly he could never tell them the truth.

"Do you mind if I smoke?" the idol said.

"What??"

"Mind if I smoke!!??" the voice boomed.

The young man told him it was fine. "Sure." A match was struck, and the young man saw that instead of this massive, stone god with the powerful, throbbing male member, he was lying next to a thin, wrinkled old man. Well, maybe not so old, but certainly wrinkled, especially to this young man.

"You're not ... you're not ... you're ... not!" the young man said.

"So? What did you expect? Hercules?" the idol's voice countered. "Listen, it gets really boring inside that idol waiting for some young chicken to come along. It wasn't bad, was it? I usually give satisfaction, right?"

The young man had to admit that was true. "I just never thought sex with an idol would end up like this," he said.

"You should see me in the morning. You think I'm disappointing now? But at least I gave you the answer to all your questions."

"You did?"

"Sure, baby." And the old man entered him again, this time slower, rhythmically, with more attentions to details, so that the young man got more out of it, too. Then the old man whispered something into the young man's ear, something the young man never, ever forgot. And with that, the old man disappeared.

The next evening, the young man's friends wanted to know all about his quest for the idol's answers. And the young man lied to them just as he promised himself he would do. He told how the great idol had spoken powerfully to him, and given him every answer. "Amazing," his clever friends said. They started to make up smart little ditties in his honor, and passed the hookah back and forth, noshing on dates and sweet meats, and staying up most of the night, even after the young man, now fired with ambition, had gone to sleep.

Then the next afternoon, his friends borrowed an oxcart and journeyed out to see the idol themselves. They were about half a dozen in number, and they were a loud, but humorous group. They alighted in front of the temple and walked together down the long passageway to the idol's reception room. There, the idol seemed gracious to them, and they all smiled at him, and he, through his bland, stone features, seemed to smile back. Then one by one, they praised the idol's generosity and intelligence, and left gifts for him. But the idol did not speak, and none of them had the courage to visit the idol in the dead of night.

But the young man did just as he thought he would: he rose way above his born station in life, and became secretary to the Prime Minister of Egypt, who reported directly to the Pharaoh. People admired and envied the young man's good fortune. They asked him many, many times the secret of his success. But he never answered them, and only gave them the same genial, neutral facial expression which he'd seen the idol make. Of course, people always interpreted this expression kindly.

But every night, before he went to sleep, the young man remembered the last words the "idol," who had met him in the dark, had spoken to him thusly:

"It is easy, young man, to discover the 'clay feet' of an idol. The real secret, my young friend, is to understand just how far those clay feet can take him."

"Well, how d' ya like that story?" my kindly host said to me.

I remembered telling him it was wonderful and nodding my head. A moment later, I finished my coffee, and then began to search out my host's own *idol* under his robe. He smiled and led me back to the satin sheets of his bedroom.

THE WHOLE PERSON

꒦

I got a call from Devlin that March. It was an early spring in New York, and it seemed that the city, even under the concrete, was stirring to life. I was feeling good about things, and although I hadn't heard from him in several weeks, just the sound of his voice got me excited. I was still in bed—alone this time—and my throat and head felt knotted with sleep when he spoke. He called me from his office and as usual made some comment about the fact that I hadn't got out of bed yet. "You people down there never get jumping till noon!" I could see his handsome, preppy face speaking into the phone, the funny smirk he had when his cheeks dimpled.

"Why you call when you know I'm gonna be in bed?" I slurred.

He told me that gave him a charge. Was I alone? Yes. What did he look like, young and pretty, or older and hunky? I told him he was young, hunky, and invisible. I started jerking off while we talked. I wanted my hands around his dick. It was fat, short, kind of meaty. I saw his large furry nuts. I wanted his dick in my mouth. I was tired of talking already and just wanted to suck his cock.

He stopped for a moment Then he said: "Would you go with me to Dayton tomorrow?"

"Dayton?"

"Yeh. Ohio. Don't think about it, just say yes. It's a relaxing way to spend a long weekend. We'll be alone in a decent hotel. There's a very good steak restaurant in town. There's ..."

Why Dayton? I asked. I tried to plug him for more information, but couldn't get any more. It was a business trip and everything would be "taken care of." He needed my company he told me. His voice took on that slight, boyish, pleading tone that I couldn't turn down. Mentally I began to get ready for the trip. A neighbor downstairs could take my mail, feed my cat, etc. "Should I meet you at your place?" No. "Don't go near Beekman Place, and we can't meet at my office." (That was no problem: I'd never been to his office.)

"There's a Florsheim shoe store at the corner of Fifty-Seventh Street and Madison Avenue."

"Near the Fuller Building, the one with all the galleries?" I asked

"Yes, meet me in front at five thirty tomorrow. I won't be late."

It got cold that night and the next day I felt chilled to the bone while I waited, a speck, really, in rush hour on this crowded, very glamorous corner of Manhattan. It was one of the centers of the art world and the Uptown money world, and they both met there. For a second I lost myself watching very busy people pass me, then a large, deep blue Cadillac for hire drew up in front of me.

"Glad you could make it," Dev said as he jumped out. He wore a light weight, gray wool suit from Dunhill, the waist slightly nipped in. A very discrete, window-pane check ran through it. I was wearing jeans and a pea-coat. He formally shook my hand, like we were posing for photos, then he took my small overnight bag, threw it in the back, and we got in. He told the driver to go straight up, and we got to see all of Madison Avenue as it became less ritzy and finally settled into East Harlem.

"Want a drink?" he asked. There was a cold chest, and Dev took out some vodka and quickly, like we were in his living room, stirred up two Gibsons, onions and all. I relaxed, then he whispered to me, "I'd like you to be very careful with this driver. Not a word about Dayton. We're going to Philadelphia and catching a plane from there."

Why Philly, I wanted to ask, and what was so special about this driver? I looked ahead, past the glass partition. He looked inoffensive enough, big, in a rumpled, black uniform, driver's cap squushed down. I could see a lot of him in the mirror. Big, bruised face and hands, the kind of face that lost teeth from fights up in the Bronx.

"You got some place special you want to go in Philadelphia, Mr. Hanson?"

Devlin told him the Rittenhouse Square Hotel, then turned out the reading light in the back and drew his head over towards me and started to doze off. I pulled him onto my lap and pulled my hands through his thick hair. I was sure the driver couldn't see in the dark and if he could—well, everything had a price, so why not some pleasure to go with it? It was going to be a long night; I knew it. I unbuttoned my fly and let my cock flop out next to Devlin's cheek. He pretended to be asleep, then started to lick it into action, and took it softly in his mouth. A shudder of pleasure went through both of us. His tongue found the small platinum ring he'd inserted a few months back into my foreskin. He flicked at the ring back and forth, wetting it with his lips; the Cadillac easily slipped into the heavy traffic of the New Jersey Turnpike. The driver stopped for a toll ticket. I was sure he could see everything going on in the back—or at least see that something was going on in the back. I'd unbuttoned most of Dev's shirt and was playing with his tits as he sucked me. Things got hotter; I carefully unzipped his fly, reached into his briefs, and slowly jerked him off—sometimes wetting my left hand with my saliva, sometimes with his. I'd never done anything like this, but it did give me some sort of insight into the lifestyles of the rich and naughty. I spotted the driver's face in the mirror. It was cold. Ice cold. He never cracked any smile, or showed any interest.

In Philadelphia, we took a cab for the airport, got an Eastern flight, and a little less than two hours later got off in Dayton. I started to feel dazed, but Dev took it in stride. He made jokes about going around his elbow to get to his thumb. He pulled out an airport rent-a-car reservation, and we got into a large Buick, brought to us by an attractive young man from Hertz. The young man smiled a lot, gave Mr. Hanson the keys, and helped us put our bags in. Dev did not travel light, I noticed. I guessed all the stock-broker drag added weight; but he did know how to get help when he needed it.

"You'll be in Suite 303," the woman at the Chevalier Motor Hotel said. She asked my name, but Devlin told her there was no need to register me as well. She smiled and said, very matter-of-factly, "I understand." I was not terribly impressed by the place. It was way out of Dayton, spread out like a miniature shopping center. The grounds looked like just after the Bomb. She apologized and told us they'd just opened, also that one of the VIP suites had just been prepared for Mr. Hanson. Devlin smiled, all dimples. A cute-as-sin, corn-fed boy picked up Dev's bags, tossed my single overnight on top, and carried them onto the elevator to the suite. He carefully placed everything on one of the two double beds and asked if we needed help unpacking.

"Maybe undressing," Dev said and winked. The boy pretended he hadn't heard. Dev gave him several bucks, and he left.

I had already begun to strip out of my Levis. The bellboy must have spotted that I wasn't wearing underwear, because I couldn't seem to get rid of what we used to call a boner. I grabbed Dev and began to tear off his clothes—tie, shirt, belt, the whole deal.

He laughed. No words. It was just going to be good sex. And real, real soon, rather than later.

Naked, we both charged into the bathroom. It was a large, deluxe affair with a whirlpool, a shower, and the usual onyx, porcelain stuff to make you know they were serious about your money. We got into the whirlpool, turning it on just hot enough. After we settled in, Dev came over to me, and in the hot, rumbling water, sat on my dick. I grabbed him, bent him towards me, and chewed on his tough, little nipples. He wrapped his legs around me. I picked him up by his ass and moved him sopping wet onto the rug in the front sitting room. I pulled out of him for a moment and turned on the TV and turned the sound all the way down. The reflections of the colors spilt all over the dark room, like a fireplace.

I went back to him and put my tongue in his sweet, firm ass and worked it around until I couldn't stand it any longer. Then I just fucked the hell out of him while I told him how much I liked doing it. A few seconds later, he came, jerking off on me, and I caught some of it in my mouth. I felt like I'd overeaten, although I hadn't eaten in quite a while. I was just tired and completely satisfied, the way I only got after sex. I didn't care if we were in Dayton—we could have been on the moon.

We cleaned off some in the shower, then went to bed. It was somewhere between midnight and one. It had been a long day for me. I dozed right off. I can't remember any dreams, but I know that somewhere in the middle of the night, Dev got out of bed, changed into jeans, a polo, and a brown suede jacket. He said something to me, and I kept saying, "Yes, yes, yes," then I went back to sleep.

The phone rang the next morning at nine. "Mr. Hanson?" a boy at the desk said. "Your wake up call." I thanked him and then realized Dev wasn't there. The room suddenly felt very strange and cold. My bare feet sank into a very thick carpet. By the TV I saw a note. "Business. Very early. Have a good time. Room Service. Use the gym. Use my name whenever. Dev."

I wondered what kind of business could begin that early, then rang for room service and had breakfast sent in. Bacon and eggs came, with a mushy croissant, canned orange juice and coffee. I called the desk again. The clerk told me they had a complete gym for people in the VIP suites, just show the key.

The gym really was very luxe, especially for some one used to New York YMCA's. I got a massage from an older Swedish guy who knew what he was doing. Then feeling about ten years younger, I dove into the pool. It was almost Olympic sized, and quite empty. I did ten laps and started to feel like those wires that get too crossed up in my brain were finally getting untangled. It was a real moment of complete relaxation and I fed on it while

I went back into the large, tiled showers. I let the needle current of hot, pulsating water hit me, and closed my eyes. I was feeling no pain at all, when a cold hand suddenly started dripping water over my back.

I turned slightly and opened my eyes. A young, naked, very trim man stood in front of me. All shoulders; strong feet; swimmer's legs. His face almost brushed mine. His cold shower dripped onto me. Water sheeted down his firm, tapered belly, onto his wild, young cock, down his balls, his knees, his calves again. I watched it. Smiled.

I began to tingle. He was too close to me and I really had to push myself back from touching him, running my hands—maybe even my mouth—over him He looked like he was made out of very shiny silver foil. "Your soap!" he shouted to me. "Can I use some of your soap? Mine's gone!"

I told him he could use anything he wanted, and I would even help. He didn't even blink. I started to wonder, was Dayton really like this? Was I really in Dayton? He took a great gob of hot, syrupy soap from my shower dispenser and started to spread it over his body. He stood away from his cold water and came closer again to me. When he bent over away from me to get to his legs, I started to massage some of the soap into his back. There was no one else in the showers. I reached down and began working on his crotch. I rubbed lather into his firm, almost cold balls, and then onto his cock. He was cut; the head was thick and kind of velvety. It got warmer and bigger in my hands. I ran my fingers over his full shaft. His dick lengthened and popped out straight in front of him.

My heart pounded. I realized that I had brought things to a place I couldn't control. Suppose Dev was now back in the suite? A moment later two business types who'd been playing squash until their pacemakers were ready to fritz came in. They gave us a funny look. I wondered what was wrong—they'd never seen two guys full of soap and hard-ons before? I decided before they called up the Pat Robertson brigade to ask him up.

His name was Stephen and I found out in the elevator that he was a private member of the gym. He wasn't staying at the Chevalier. We exchanged some short pleasantries until we got back to the suite, where there was still no sign of Devlin. The maids, I saw, had come in and done an assaultive job of cleaning up the place. It was in the sort of immaculate order you expected in convents.

A few seconds later, we had our clothes off. I knew this kid was no kid. He was very much a man. He knew everything and maybe some things I didn't. Besides having such a lovely body and cock, he had a beautiful mouth and I couldn't get enough of it. I was nuts about his mouth—in fact, I wanted my nuts in his mouth. I wanted to kiss him and have him suck me at the same time. I was *that* nuts about his mouth. Everything became an extension of something else. One moment my mouth would go to his, then down to his balls; then I'd feel his soft, wet tongue reaching for the head of my dick; or my own mouth all over his shaft, and it was all like we were exploring each other this way, going further and further.

Nothing had prepared me for finding this beautiful man next to me in the showers at just the right moment. I wanted to have him—every part of him—maybe even all at once; to kiss the whole person, taste him completely, sexually, experience all of him. He started to vibrate while he knelt over me and I pressed his dick into my mouth. The muscles in his belly and ass quivered. I fed on more and more of his cock. My lips finally pressed the hairs next to his balls.

He asked, "Do you like this?" He smiled. He knew I did. I was getting closer and closer, just from the heat of sucking *his* cock

I started to play with my dick. He pulled out of my mouth. Suddenly he said to me—just out of nowhere—"Would you like to get tied up?"

I laughed. I thought, Jesus, bondage, here in Dayton? I could hardly take the idea seriously, which only goes to show you how much I know. So I thought, why not?

He took some leather thongs out of his jacket pocket, and tied me down, fastening my hands to the front legs of one of the beds. I started to think: this is *really* crazy, but the whole time he was doing this, he kept me very excited, so I have to admit, I really wasn't doing much thinking at all. I was crazy with lust for him. He was beautiful enough with his young, athletic body to do a lot for me in the excitement department. He tied one of the thongs around my balls. I thought I was going to cream right then. Then he began carefully to tie my legs together.

I watched him doing this. He was completely hard, and obviously really turned on. His cock, amazingly enough, got even bigger. It mushroomed out. Then suddenly I started thinking again—here I am, in a strange hotel, with a strange person. I'm older than he is. And stronger. I knew that. I'm smarter, too. I wasn't sure, but I could just tell it.

But if I was so damned smart, why'd I let some one I didn't know tie me up?

He began whipping me with another thong. It was actually a kind of leather tassel and reminded me of a cat-o-nine-tails. It was light and very exciting. Everytime the rawhide went over my body, cold, raw delicious prickles of nerves shot up my legs. I felt the sensations run over my tight belly. It was a funny feeling. My tits hardened, like they'd been exposed to cold.

My cock got, like they say, "rock" hard. I mean *hard*, very, very—almost painfully—hard. The tip was on fire. He brushed the leather whip over the tip of it, just grazing the hole several times. He smiled as he saw my body flutter from every jerk of my dick. I started whimpering like a dog. I couldn't help it. I lost control of myself. I begged him to make me come.

He started to chuckle. Now he was in control. I told him I was tired of playing, and he really started laughing. The sound of it rattled the room. It went up my neck and I could feel the electric energy of his laugh getting to me.

He started to feed his cock into my mouth. I sucked urgently at it, while my dick slapped back and forth in the air. I took his fat dick into me. Huge rushes of heat kept shooting through me. He licked his fingers and started to play with me, pushing and pinching my tits, then rubbing the head of my cock with his spit-wet hands. I was unable to change anything, to speed it along or slow it down, to control any part of me until a complete sexual explosion fired through my body. It began just below my navel and traveled on a road of raw nerves through my ass, then into my balls, and finally, like the wet-glow of a volcano, shot out of my near bursting cock.

For a second, I thought I'd come on the ceiling. I felt it trickling all over me, running in thick white spurts down my belly. Then I realized that Stephen, too, had come and had shot all over me.

I stopped breathing, closed my eyes, and let the whole, wild energy of the orgasm run its course through me. I was still tied down. The knots began to hurt, rub me just a bit. I looked up. He got closer to me, put his face next to mine, and told me to relax. I did. He untied the thongs. I was free of them, rubbed my hands and feet, then stretched out on the rug. "Why don't you come over here?" I said to him.

He answered that he would in a minute. I know I should have watched what was going on, but I suddenly felt wiped out. I hadn't expected that kind of sex, so early, at least. I closed my eyes again. When I opened them, I realized it was a real mistake.

He had disappeared, as suddenly as he had appeared in the gym. I jumped up. Suppose he'd stolen something? How could I explain it to Dev? I looked around the room, but everything was there. I felt very relieved, and just chalked it up as another strange event in Dayton. I got into the shower, then toweled off. I had on a pair of briefs when I heard a knock at the door. "May we come in a moment, Mr. Hanson?" a man asked.

Cautiously, I opened the door. I wanted to explain that Mr. Hanson wasn't there, and frankly I didn't know where he was; but it was getting damn close to lunch and I was tired of waiting for him—when suddenly three men rushed me. Like a truck. Some one pushed a cloth doused with chemicals right into my nose. Instant nausea. My legs went watery. The blood left my head. I fell straight to the floor.

"The plans you stole, Mr. Hanson. Where are the plans?" I tried to focus on this man who looked like a side of beef. He kept questioning me. I wasn't

Mr. Hanson, I told him, and I didn't know what he was talking about. Suddenly, in my wacked-out state—which was like gazing through several sheets of rippled glass—I saw some one enter the room. "Are you through with me?" Stephen asked.

"We're through," the side of beef answered. "You don't tell anyone what's gone on here, okay? You don't tell nobody, right?"

Stephen shook his head They started to throw some clothes at me and I knew I had to get into them. I managed to get on my jeans, and a flannel shirt, but it was difficult. Everything bewildered me. I felt stupid and impotent, two feelings I'm not crazy about. My limbs felt too Jello-y to resist. I started crying—actually, it was like some one else was crying—and I was only watching. Most of me was in a black-out, in a fog. "Who are you?" I shouted to Stephen, as he watched me passively. "Who the hell are you?"

He didn't answer, but just disappeared.

They seemed to know the whole layout of the Chevalier. They led me through a back exit, and we passed several boys in uniform who acted like this was just a normal event—three, very beefy types dragging someone either very drugged or drunk out the back. I passed the kid who'd brought in our bags. They smiled and gave him a couple of dollars. Then we got out into an overcast day, in the rear employees' parking lot.

They threw me in the back of a van. After several miles of flat highway, the van turned off the road. Things got bumpier, then stopped. They opened up the back.

"Alley-oop!" one shouted; two pulled me out. Mr. Beef, who I guessed was the Boss, injected something into my arm. I became instantly alert. "You got a lotta talking to do, Mr. Hanson," he growled. "We wanna hear it all."

In the distance I saw an old, abandoned farm house, surrounded by flat, open fields. With his two friends on either side, they made sure I got there. The Boss spoke to me. "Y' know, Mr. Hanson, when you play around with some people, you get burned bad. You spy on another country, maybe diplomats get you out. But this industrial spying—you're fucking around with computers. And computers mean a *lot* of money."

At the door, he reminded me, "Mr. Hanson, you've made a very bad mistake."

I agreed. I'd done it, and I wasn't even Mr. Hanson. Suddenly I hated Devlin very much. They switched on a small overhead light, tied me up, and literally threw me down a short flight of stairs into a dark basement. For a moment, all was extremely quiet. Then the basement door clicked closed.

I could hear them upstairs going on about what they were going to do with me. They were going to make me talk, then—somewhere—soon, I was going to be fertilizing one of those fields in Ohio. My blood ran cold. I kept breathing deeply to keep from peeing in my jeans. Everything had seemed so unreal, so nightmarish. I wasn't even sure how I'd managed to dress. In the dark, my hands ran down my jeans; then I realized I wasn't wearing socks.

They were returning. The basement door snapped back open. The Boss stomped in, alone. He exploded: "You know what we're going to do with you, Mr. Hanson?"

"For the last time," I pleaded, "I'm not Mr. - "

"HE'S NOT—" Dev's voice rang out. He moved out from behind several large kegs. I looked at him; my mouth fell open. Calmly he raised a small pistol, just slightly.

"Mr... Han-son..." the Boss said. His face dropped. Devlin nailed him right there. The pistol went off with a sharp, vicious crack. Then the large body fell down the short flight of stairs, until it landed in front of me. I looked down. "He's dead, alright," Dev said.

I swallowed hard. "Why'd you do this to me?" I asked.

"Shhh." He ran up the stairs, then fired two shots into the door. A moment later, I heard the van speed off. He came back down and untied me. "Where's Stephen?" he asked. I told him I had no idea. I didn't even know who this Stephen was.

"You mean you let just anyone tie you up, fuck your mouth—the whole deal?"

"How'd you know all this?"

"I can't explain it right now," he said. He grabbed me, kissed me. "God, I'm glad you're okay. You know, I think I love you, even more than I let on."

I suddenly laughed. We went up the stairs. I was frightened but there was no one in the house. Dev assured me once the Boss was dead, they'd scram. "Come on," Dev smiled, as casually as if we were just leaving a bar. Still dazed, I followed him. The rented Buick was hidden about half a mile away in a grove of trees. We got in and he drove back to the house. "Stay for a sec," he said, the engine still running. I must have looked alarmed, so he gave me a quick, reassuring peck on the cheek. He got out; I heard the basement door slam again as he jumped back into the car. He threw the car into reverse and we were out of there. A moment later, the bottom floor of the house blew out. I swallowed hard. He drove me back to the Chevalier. I went in, got our bags, and the same boy helped me pile them into the car. I gave him five bucks for a tip. He thanked me.

"You like Stephen?" Dev asked as we drove back towards the airport.

"What does that have to do with it?" I asked. I was furious, still scared and fairly nauseated. "Was this some sort of test you put me through, Dev?

I realize now I don't know you at all."

He smiled with that open, disarming, dimpled smile. "It's hard to know the whole person, isn't it? I do what I do for many reasons. Money is certainly one of them. Sometimes, it's so that the right people get a chance. These computer plans, for instance, belong to a client of Stephen's. We both knew there was a plot to steal them—I just worked against that plot, that's all."

"So you didn't steal them?"

He shook his head no. He'd intercepted a drop-off of the plans at five o' clock that morning. "They're in the right hands now," he told me, and grabbed my hand. "Just like you are."

"You almost got me killed," I said.

"Hell, you should've seen what happened at five this morning! I met Stephen, intercepted the drop-off, followed these goons around so we'd know where they'd bring you. Gee, what a morning—worse than playing half a dozen games of squash at my club."

"Is that what that was—just worse than," I sputtered, "*squash*?"

"We play squash to kill, Smoky."

"You rich bastards—you almost got *me* killed," I growled.

Dev's face dropped. It was one of those rare moments when he realized I wasn't going to play *his* game. He stopped the car, and I saw that he was shaking now. I turned to him and touched his face gently.

"It's okay, Dev. I don't hate you. I'm sorry what I said about rich bastards."

"I would never get you killed. Never!"

"So what about Stephen?" I asked.

He smiled again, and started the car. "Gorgeous, isn't he?" That Devlin Hanson smirk went back into his face, the smile that was coy and full of nerves. It was a smile I could barely resist.

Several flat miles later, he turned the car off the road to the airport. I thought we were just going back. Dev shook his head no, and headed for the other side of Dayton, to an empty shopping center where there was a bar, its parking lot filled with cars. As soon as we walked in, I knew it was a gay bar. Dev and I got through the crowd and the smoke. Suddenly, in a corner by himself, I saw Stephen. Dev went up to him and Stephen smiled at me. Dev led the two of us back out to the Buick. "Do you want to spend the next two nights at Stephen's house?"

"What?"

"He's rented a place out in the country, near Antioch. It's completely secluded." He smiled.

I looked over at Stephen, the picture of perfect innocence. Then suddenly—from *who* could guess what—I felt myself going wobbly. Stephen

118

grabbed me, and Dev opened the door to the car. I got in. Stephen fell on top of me, kissing me, quickly running his hands inside my flannel shirt. I felt myself getting hotter, smoking like a gun for him. Just the sight of him had caused me to lose my balance. I shot my tongue into his mouth. He returned it, then pressed his lips to my neck. My hand went into his hair. I pulled him closer to me.

"You'd better get into your car," Dev said to Stephen. I let him go.

Stephen straightened himself up. "You have something for me?"

"I almost forgot." Dev passed him the revolver. "Better get rid of it. I fixed it so that no one's going to be able to get to the body. I'm sure his goons won't get the cops involved."

We followed Stephen's red Datson sedan onto the highway. I said to Dev, "Now, tell me all about Stephen."

"Don't worry. He's a smart—and quite rich—kid, but you can trust him."

"I hope more than I can trust you," I said.

"Sorry, Smokes, but there was no way I could let you in on all this. Believe me, I wish I could—but I couldn't. My company can't even find out. Stephen's an old friend of mine. Okay, the truth is we were lovers once, so I did it for him. There are certain things you just don't let go of—know what I mean?"

I told him I did. Devlin Hanson was certainly one of them.

Dev looked relieved. The dimples in his smile didn't look so hard. He took my hand and softly kissed it. "Good. Stephen's nice, isn't he? Now, didn't I tell you we were going to have a very relaxing weekend in Dayton?"

THE BOATHOUSE

Spence and I were tooling over the Causeway over Lake Pontchartrain—the huge, shallow, salt-water lake that disconnects New Orleans from the rest of Louisiana, if not the world, and that always makes you feel like a flea suddenly dunked into a wax-paper cup of cherry soda. There's something thick and sweet about so much salt water flattened out under hot air, surrounded by palm trees and bayous full of Creole shacks or an occasional mansion. We were going to one of the mansions, owned by Rollo Benedict. Rollo was a king pin in the beauty business out this way. He owned a genuine compound near Magdalene, LA (just below Bogalusa, a town whose name seemed to drip Spanish moss; how could you not have a good time in a place called *Bogalusa* or even Magdalene, for that matter?).

Spence was the man I worked for. Spence Butler, ex-football jock, now side-of-beef flabby, but with good thighs—I always said, "Spence, you got good thighs"—and a sweetheart, really, though always a big mouth. Spence was at the wheel, going on a mile-a-minute about the meeting with Rollo. The idea of this pow-wow was to plan the big beauty convention in July. It was now June and hot enough for anyone who had a hankering for the tropics to be perfectly happy in Louisiana. Rollo's idea was to get 10,000 hairdressers from all over the South East into New Orleans in July, before they

121

split in August and spent all their money someplace else.

Spence was yapping away as usual. Spence was as straight as a pin (okay, even pins get bent now and then, but for my purposes, he was as straight as a pin) and he believed in the beauty business the way that in Iran they believe in Allah. "Here's the deal. Dig? Mondrian (the name of our classy, beauty promotion company) will provide all back-up promo services. Organize. Programs. Material. The whole deal. Rollo's company puts up the place, the money, and the samples. You gotta have samples. You listenin' to me?"

I was not. I had learned through the last ten months of self-preservation at Mondrian that if I listened to Spence, I'd just go crazy. So I didn't. I would nod my head, agree with everything, and look out the window at the Lake, when I wasn't agreeing. I told Spence months ago that just 'cause I agreed with him didn't mean that I was going to do what he said, anyway.

"So, what are you going to do, when we get to Magdalene?" Spence asked.

It took me about half a second to come up with the correct answer: "Suck all the dick I can."

Spence was so amused he almost let go of the wheel. About ten minutes later, we were there. I'd never been to Rollo's compound before, but I could get used to any place with this much money behind it. You went off the main road into a smaller, oyster-shell drive, palms on both sides, then turned into a circular driveway, and there it was: Chez Rollo. Huge. White. Lots of wood and great windows. The living room was big enough to have the Louisiana Democratic Convention in. Behind the house was the guesthouse, where the gossip was that Rollo put his ex-wives—there were three of them—and then the boathouse. The boathouse was connected to a dock that went way out into the bayou that connected, I was sure, to the Lake again.

I took one look and I was happy. Spence introduced me to Rollo, whom I'd met several times but never when both of us were sober, and Rollo offered us drinks, something to eat, and then several "proscribed substances" that could have gotten any of us arrested almost any place except hereabouts. We ate some and drank some, and then Spence and Rollo began the arduous work of hashing out who was going to do what to whom at Beauty Louisiana, the upcoming show.

I sat and watched a while, then realized that Spence and Rollo—you must understand Rollo was not wearing a shirt and Spence was trying to sit there with a pocket calculator he couldn't use—needed a writer there, even one with my estimable talents, like a turtle needs a mobile home. I decided this was now high time for me to investigate the rest of the place. I gave Spence what had become a pre-arranged signal, tapping my forehead twice,

122

and he said, "Smokes, why don't you take yourself a walk out back? Look at the boathouse." And I did.

Rollo was real nice about it. He offered to show me around the place himself, but I didn't want to interrupt the meeting, and I knew that I was basically there as some sort of decoration or maybe ballast. Spence and I had worked out a scheme whereby whenever somebody offered us something we wouldn't go for, he would just say, "You know Smoky will never stand for this." That was basically why I was there, not to stand for things, and I was getting itchy to look around anyway.

I went through a long hallway, trying not to appear *too* nosy as I inspected various rooms in the house. For a guy who wore his gold jewelry by the pound, Rollo did not have bad taste. The furniture was large, simple, and it augmented the black velvet paintings of nude ladies well. Finally, there in the back, through a TV den big enough to house several families, I saw the boathouse.

I opened the glass door and went out into the thick, un-air-conditioned air. The small building—right on the water—looked so beautiful, shimmering, yellow, in the heat. I climbed up the stairs to the dock. For a second, I wondered what sort of boats Rollo had. I knew he had a couple of yachts that had escaped his various divorces. I tried the door, but it was locked. There were no windows at eye-level, only a few vents up near the roof, so I couldn't look in.

I felt very frustrated, but there was nothing to do except make a turn off the right on the dock, and walk out to the end, past the boathouse. The dock extended maybe half a city block, and there was room to tie up six or seven good sized boats. When I got out to the end, I could see what might have been the other bank of the bayou.

It was thick with shoulder-high grasses and palmetto trees waving in the heat. On second thought, I might have been looking at several, small islands of heavier swamp. Out there it was hard to tell where the land and the water ended.

It was hot as blazes, out there at close to high noon, in the middle of all this almost stagnant water. The heat was starting to make me dizzy. I felt suddenly lost, out of focus. I knew I'd better get back into the house and try to lie down, but on the other hand, I wasn't ready for Spence and Rollo, either.

I hurried back to the boathouse, which now really glared from its bright coat of fresh enamel, yellow paint, then I walked around it, on the rim of the dock, until I was out of the sun. There was a small ledge of shadow—at about one in the afternoon, you didn't get much shade—and I stood against it. I really wished the damn boathouse had been open; then suddenly I realized the smartest thing to do was just take my clothes off, dive into the water, and then come up inside it. Since the boathouse was the same level as the dock, I knew the water had to be fairly deep even here, closer to the house.

I took off my loafers and socks, and then stripped off my chinos, white shirt, and my striped, silk preppy tie. The tie had been my idea. If you can't outspend these people, at least try to outdress them.

I felt wonderful being buck naked, and realized how dangerously hot I'd been. The silky, black hairs on my chest were soaked in perspiration, and my cock felt thick from heat. The base of it was swollen a bit, and my pubic hair was wet and tangled. My balls hung low from the heat. I went over to the side, and knelt down a bit to scoop some water up in my hand. Then I splashed some of it on my crotch, just to cool my nuts off; then I dove in.

The water was dark; not dirty, really, just dark. It was like swimming in coffee. I closed my eyes, and felt my way under the boathouse, and then carefully—very carefully, with my hands groping over my head—came up.

It seemed pitch black in the boathouse, but much cooler, and after a few minutes the blackness subsided and I realized that it was simply dimly lit. It was smart not to have windows, because the darkness kept the place cooler. I swam up to a ledge that ran around the sides of the building—actually the inside of the dock—and hoisted myself up on it. I stood up uneasily and started to walk on the ledge.

I had that wonderful, kid-like, naked feeling that made me feel I was getting away with something. It was like the feeling I used to have when I'd excuse myself from my parents' parties—I was just a kid then—to go jerk off in the bathroom. One time, I remember, Mark, a friend of theirs, a seminarian, yet, came in and joined me. But I think that should be another story.

I walked carefully around the ledge. Rollo did have a big boat. My wet feet made a splatting, sucking noise on the wooden ledge, and my cock kept flapping from side to side in unison with it. To increase the pleasure of all this, I started playing with the head of my cock, rubbing it between the wet, cold palms of my hands.

Rollo's boat—a huge, pink and white yacht that Spence told me was called—dig this—"Beauty Queen"—was the only one housed. I felt disappointed, but I wanted to take a real look at her. I've always liked big boats, or any boats for that matter. I found a light switch on the wall.

I flicked it on, then suddenly heard a man's voice say, "Turn that off!" It scared the shit out of me. I mean, I was pretty much intruding and I knew I was standing there fully naked, and half-hard. I flicked the light right off. Then I saw this very attractive young man—maybe twenty-one or twenty-two—walking barefoot on the ledge towards me. I had to look twice just to convince myself I wasn't dreaming this, because he was also almost naked, too, except for a pair of Jockey shorts. I was naked, period. I knew at this

124

point that things were either very bad, or going to get better and better.

He gave me this funny, half-smirk smile, and asked me what I was doing there. I told him I was just taking a look around, and tried to take more of a look at him, without getting too excited. He was a pretty blond creature, and I was sure that in the light his eyes were really blue, or maybe green. Then he really smiled at me. "You always take a look around stark naked?" I told him that my clothes were beyond the wall, on the other side of the dock. Since the boathouse was locked, I came in from under.

As I tried to explain most of the immediate details to him, without mentioning either Spence or Rollo, I picked out more details about him. He had a young, slender chest, broad shoulders, and small, hot little tits that were causing my mouth to salivate ridiculously. He also had an amazing amount of really sweet, funky blond hair on his upper chest, that swirled around his nipples, and then ran into a deep dish in his navel. I knew I was really losing control, and my dick was now quite hard. This didn't seem to faze him, so I pretended just to forget about it—that is, if any human male can do such a thing. Then playfully, I pointed to his skivvies, and suddenly put my right index finger into the waistband, and snapped it against his taut little stomach.

(Okay—I admit it—I can be quite playful.)

He laughed nervously. "I'm supposed to be painting the Beauty Queen, Mister, but it's so hot I just decided to take a nap here for a while." He asked me not to tell anyone that I'd caught him goofing off in the boathouse, and I told him that I'd cross my heart. I felt that who ever he was—probably one of Rollo's many hired hands—he probably felt self-conscious stripped down to his underwear, and I decided the best thing to do was to make sure he got his underwear off as quickly as possible.

I lowered myself back into the water, and asked him if he wanted to join me. At first he said he wasn't sure if he could do that. "I'd really better get back to painting this boat," he said, shyly. Finally he agreed it was much cooler in the water. His Jockeys were soaked through with sweat, so I could see the head of his heavy cock pressing against the soft cotton. He jumped right in, Jockeys on, and came up next to me.

I told him that was no fair, and pointed to his shorts. He could only smile, and I wondered if he knew I had a full hard-on in the dark water. I got closer to him, so that the head of my dick brushed against his naked thighs. He just smiled more, and certainly didn't swim away, or melt. I reached in, under the leg band of his shorts, and felt his dick. He was hard already.

For a second, I thought I was going to cum right then.

As they say in the movies, "Wow..."

His cock was really large to be attached to such a sweet, slender, young

125

thing. I ran my left hand up the shaft of his dick until it reached the thick ridge of its head. I decided at this point that there was no use in being anything but completely honest. "I like men with thick heads on their dicks," I whispered to him. A second later, I had his Jockeys off, and threw them onto the deck of the boathouse.

He didn't say a word, but kept smiling while I grabbed him around the waist. We were both squishy with salt water. I kissed him full on the mouth, while kneading the firm cheeks of his ass, and then I dove down into the water. I found his balls down there, and started licking them under the dark water. His balls had tightened up, but relaxed, and I sucked at them, without getting a bit of water in my mouth. You might consider this a minor talent. Then with what breath I had left, I went to the head of his dick and got as much as I could of it into my mouth. It reminded me of a large, sweet, Creole tomato.

I had to come up for a second. We grabbed each other. I was slightly out of breath, then we both went under. We had our eyes open, and I could see the hull of the Beauty Queen. He grabbed my hand, and we went under the boat to the other side, and then resurfaced. I couldn't keep my hands off him, and had started eating his ass while he pulled himself up onto the boathouse deck. I got out of the water, and we climbed into the boat.

It was too hot even to go into the cabins. We were both quickly covered in perspiration, so we went back to the rear deck of the boat. It was cooler. My heart started racing from the heat—and just general stimulation. A moment later, we were lying on the stern, above the motor, and I was slowly, deliciously, sucking his dick, while he grabbed one of my tits with one hand, and caressed my hot balls with the other. Then we eased ourselves around, until he had my dick in his mouth, too. I thought I was in hog heaven.

It all happened too fast and too wonderful. I knew that at any second, I was going to spurt my cookies all over the place. I wasn't sure how close I was to cumming, but he was so good at eating my dick that I couldn't hold back any longer. I let him have a great load of cum, and tried really hard at the same time to get him off.

"I want to fuck you," he said to me, and I knew that this lovely young man sure meant business. He got up and walked bare-assed and full-dicked back into the first cabin. A second later, he came back with a jar of hand creme. Using the long fingers of both hands, he greased me and his cock up. I bent over the stern, and he stuck that wonderful, large thing right into me. Slowly at first, and then with a regular, swelling, hot rhythm that just blew all of my circuits out from the inside. Even though I'd already cum, I ended up having a second go-round when he did. He had a great, throbbing, full-steam orgasm, bucking back and forth in spasms of release. I followed him, jerking myself off with a couple of strokes.

We collapsed together like a bunch of wet clothes. "That was great," I said and kissed him. Then I heard it—what a noise! Spence was shouting for me from some distance, and I knew that if he came out to the deck, he'd find my clothes, and either suspect that I had drowned or insist that Rollo unlock the boathouse.

I told him that I had to go. I didn't even know his name. He offered to unlock the back door of the boathouse but I figured it would be a lot smarter if I just got out the way I got in.

When I surfaced, Spence was standing over my clothes. He was not amused. "I thought you were going out for a walk. Not a swim. Shit, I would have got in there with you!"

I told him he'd better not. "Sometimes I play dirty," I warned. I put on my underwear and shirt, and looking fairly tacky, walked back with Spence into the house. Rollo, as usual, was nonplussed. "Everybody wants to go swimmin' in this kind o' weather, don't they?"

He led me into a humongous bath, where I took a shower and made myself look decently presentable. I had a Scotch out in the living room, where Spence and Rollo were sorting out the final elements of the beauty show deal.

I smiled and pretended to be listening to everything, as I always did. This, certainly, is another thing that writers—like psychiatrists—are always paid to do: to pretend to be listening. It was now about four thirty and the sun was lower, casting long, beautiful shadows from the bayou and the shrubs outside. A noise came in from the back, and Rollo looked up. The attractive, young blond from the boathouse appeared. Rollo smiled.

"Spence, Smoky—you haven't met Jason, have you?"

Spence got up to shake his hand. I wasn't sure what to do, but I must have had the all-time-worst Cheshire cat smile on my face. Rollo went on: "This is my son, Jason Benedict."

We left about half an hour later. Jason walked with Rollo to the car, while Spence yapped away about percent points and future grosses. Without letting them see, I unsnapped my watch and put it into my pants pocket. "I think I left my watch at the boathouse," I said.

"Jason," Rollo said, "Why don't you go see if you can find it?"

I told them we'd both go, and we hurried off to the boathouse. When I got him out of their sight, I held him and kissed him. "You're quite a surprise," I said, and promised I'd see him again.

"So, you found the watch?" Spence asked, driving out to the Causeway. I told him I had, and looked out the window. The sky was that flamingo pink it only gets in Louisiana.

"Tell me," Spence said, " Seriously, now, Smoky—what *did* you do that whole time you were out there, while Rollo and I were hashing out this deal? You weren't messin' around with that kid, were you?"

There were times I could hardly lie, even to Spence. But this was not one of them, although thank God he was driving and couldn't look me straight in the eye. So all I could do was just look slightly away from him and say, "You don't think I'm that sort of person, do you, Spence?"

At that, Spence simply chuckled very quietly to himself and said, "I hope not."

THE $\mathcal{S}$ELF-EXPRESSION FACTOR

7

I couldn't believe that the telephone was ringing at what I was sure was an indecently early hour. It wasn't. It was already almost noon. I answered. "Hi ya, honey," a heavy voice said. It was Spence Butler, my straight partner at Mondrian, our beauty promotion company. Why do straight men have to get you out of bed when you're just getting into some dream that finally fits?

"What'cha doin', darlin'?" Spence asked. Fifteen years in the beauty business had turned Spence into a perfect camp. He could still crack walnuts with his bare hands, or maybe even his thighs, but he was a real camp.

"I was having a wet dream about Jason Benedict"—a lovely young man I'd met a few weeks earlier, who just happened to turn out to be the son of our local money man.

This did not sit well with Spence, who told me in nothing flat to leave my pecker where it should be, and leave kids like Jason alone. "We got enough trouble with this beauty show without you screwin' Rollo Benedict's son."

Spence then demanded that I be at the Hilton on Canal Street in one hour. Press conference. *The Times Picayune, The New Orleans Parish Gazette,* and several no-account papers were going to be there, not to forget all the

129

local talk show "host-es and hostesses"—as Spence called them—he could strong arm into getting there. As usual, Spence would do all the talking, and I'd come along for moral support or to be some sort of class angle.

The thought was exceedingly dreary, but I pulled myself together—shit, shower, shave, coffee, blue blazer, *spanking* white shirt—how I did love that one, *spanking* white shirt—and a very preppy, dark tie. I found a cab waiting for me on Burgundy Street and St. Phillip. It was not air conditioned, and it was the first week of July, and I knew that if I so much as thought about just one of Jason's pretty, blond dick hairs, I was going to melt in this kind of New Orleans weather.

Luckily, the Hilton was revved up to mink-stole air conditioning. That is the peculiar southern habit of pushing the indoor temp up so cold your nose drops ice cycles, but it keeps the ladies comfortable in their wraps. The press conference was in a third floor meeting room. Rollo was there, looking like a million dollars or at least wearing enough gold to fool anyone. "Hi you, Sweetheart?" Rollo said to me. I flashed him a great, toothy smile, and told him I had to get a cup of coffee. "No, darlin', allow me," Rollo said. He beckoned for one of his assistants, a very burly Cajun man who was part body guard and chauffeur. When you carry around that much jewelry, you need protection, I decided. The Cajun presented me with a fresh cup, and one of those sweet smiles that made my nuts boil, despite the indoor refrigeration.

Suddenly Rollo pulled me towards him. "I guess you must be wonderin' about my son, Jason?" he whispered to me.

I smiled. Nice kid, I told him.

"Let's keep him that way," Rollo warned. He let go of my arm, and I decided that the best thing to do was to fade quickly into some woodwork.

The Press came in, my dear fellow workers of the plume, the scroll, and the word processor. They began firing questions at Spence who was a champion at complicating the simple and obliterating the complicated. In other words, don't ask for straight answers from straights. Suddenly, Miss Mandee DeBourgeois, from the TV show "Orleans Talk," asked, "What do you think is going to be the theme of this thing ya'll call 'Beauty Louisiana'?"

Spence suddenly looked lost for words. I knew he couldn't just say, "To make a whole lot o' money for us," so I decided to jump in.

130

"The *theme* of 'Beauty Louisiana,'" I said, clearing my throat, "will be"—I took a deep breath; the b.s. level was getting very thick in the room—"'The Self-Expression Factor.'"

There was a moment of heart-breaking silence, then everyone cheered. Flash bulbs fired off, and Spence broke off into one of his famous impromptu speeches on how "Self-Expression is the Natural Birthright of Every

American Lady." This was one of Spence's slip-in speeches. He could have done the same thing on Charity, Remorse, or a good blue hair rinse. Finally, the damn thing was over, and we all shook hands with the ladies and gentlemen of the Press and the Media, and watched them put away their equipment. Spence took me aside. "That was brilliant, Smoky," he said to me.

I told him that being brilliant was what I was paid to do. We walked out together. Spence told me that he and Rollo were having dinner that night. Luckily, or unluckily, I was not invited. As much as I loathed business dinners, I knew how important they were to the continuance of my weekly pay checks. In this business, who you blew was important. Speaking of which, Spence went into a quick Daddy-knows-best routine.

"About Jason. You better leave that kid alone. I don't want anything to fuck up Beauty Louisiana."

I promised I would, and took a cab back to the French Quarter. When I got home, I felt tired. I'd been up too late the night before, cavorting with some of my buddies in the bars, and the press conference had taken more out of me that I wanted to give it. I took off my clothes and hung everything up that wrinkled. It was a nice feeling, being stark naked in my small, carriage-house apartment at the end of a courtyard. I had complete privacy back there, one of the joys of life in the French Quarter.

I went out into my patio, and sat down bare-assed on one of the canvas director's chairs. I often had coffee or lunch out there when it wasn't too hot. Three huge live oak trees above cooled the place down. Suddenly, there was a ring at the gate by the street. I hesitated a bit, and the bell ringing continued. I definitely did not want company, but it could have been Spence with some sort of late-breaking news.

I snuck up to the gate, which was at the end of a very narrow passageway between a garden wall and the large house at the front of my courtyard. The wrought iron gate was covered in ivy. I asked who it was. It was Jason. I opened the gate carefully and let him in. "Let me just put on some clothes," I said. He told me he'd rather take his off. He was wearing a white poplin suit and a tie and looked so fucking southern preppy handsome my balls ached. Oh, yes, I thought. You take it off ....

We walked back to the patio. I let him know that his father had connected us. "I didn't tell him anything," he blurted out. "He's just trying to control me. He always does."

"I'd sure like to control you," I said, and began to unbutton his shirt myself. I reached in and played with his small, hard, delicious nipples. He was amazingly hairy for a young man, with the kind of silky, sweet, pale chest hairs that could destroy the resolve of much stronger men than myself. I got him into the house and peeled off his clothes like the skin of a ripe banana, till I got to his own nice banana, which I immediately stuck into my mouth, licking and stroking the thick, hard shaft from all sides.

He pulled his dick out of my mouth, then went down to suck me, too. I loved it. Then I had one of my more brilliant ideas, much nicer than a silly theme for "Beauty Louisiana."

I took him out into the courtyard. None of my neighbors—who were all gay anyway—from the big house were home.

I took out the garden hose and we began splashing each other with it. I turned it on fairly full-blast and ran it up his nuts, till they became cold and hard, and followed my mouth with that, to warm them up again. Then I kneeled under him, and ran a blast of the hose up his ass, and did the same thing with my tongue. "Why don't you fuck me?" he said, and I said why not, and went into my house and found a perfectly good rubber, some K-Y, and a snifter of cognac and came out with all of them.

I was fully hard and ready, so getting the rubber on was no problem. I sat down on one of the hard, wet flagstones in the courtyard floor and I slicked his butt up with K-Y, and then he eased his ass way down on my dick. We drank the cognac and fucked for a very long time. I pulled out a few times and sucked his long, blond cock and just when he was about to explode his cookies, I came right up his ass into the rubber.

Without touching the rubber, I went over and turned the hose off, then went back to him. I kissed him a great deal, all over his handsome face, down into his throat with my tongue. Then I got up and peeled the rubber off and tossed it into a plastic garbage bag in the kitchen. When I came back out into the courtyard, Jason looked at me very seriously. "I want to come here and live with you," he said. I closed my eyes. This was something I didn't think I could handle right then. I asked him why he wanted to do something like that. "Rollo's driving me nuts. He hates me 'cause I'm gay."

I asked him if he was sure of that. It seemed strange to me. I could understand that Rollo might not want me fucking with his son, but why should he hate Jason for being gay. Rollo was a beauty tycoon, surrounded by gay men.

Then I realized I was only fooling myself. Beauty, like any other big business, may look gay on the outside, but on the inside, where the big bucks change hands, it is a hard and very straight business. We went back into the carriage house and showered together. I felt very tender and warm towards him, and I would have been happy to sleep with him a lot, and might not even keep track of the nights. Okay, I admit it: I was falling in love with Jason Benedict. But I wasn't totally crazy. We got dressed.

"Just go back to him," I said, "until this fucking beauty show is over. Then if you feel you want to break with Rollo, we can talk about it."

I didn't see Spence for the next two days, which made me feel good. I just hoped that no one had seen me with Jason—the French Quarter being one of the world's largest phone party lines: it would be discussed in every bar on Bourbon Street in an hour. I had to lay low from Jason for the next several weeks. Every time I saw Rollo, he would give me a look that would turn my blood cold. Finally, something must have happened, because he started smiling and coming up to me, and telling me what a good job Spence and I had done to pull a large beauty convention off.

"Beauty Louisiana" came off basically the way we thought it would. We didn't get as many hairdressers as we had hoped, but it pretty much filled the New Orleans Convention Center and everybody seemed to have a good time—and they spent a lot of money. This made Rollo Benedict happy because the stylists bought huge amounts of the beauty products that he distributed, and it made Spence happy because he signed up two new clients—a big salon and a TV station—for Mondrian, our company. By any account, it should have made me happy, but it didn't.

Just making money has never made me happy, one of the great character faults in my life. At least I've been told that on more than one occasion. I was anxious about this situation with Jason, and I was getting cruised a lot by more hunky hair dressers and their wandering boyfriends than I ever knew existed.

I guess you could say that the inevitable did happen, when I met up with Everly—that was his real name, believ-*er* it or not—from a small town near Lake Charles.

He was a big, hard-boned guy, about six-foot-two. He'd been a high school football player, but never took to college and inherited a small salon from his mother in Boonville, a wide place in the road in swampy, Cajun country. I would quickly say he was not what you'd expect a country beautician to be like, but then maybe he was. Out there, where the rivers flattened out and alligators crawled up to your back porch for breakfast (and sometimes breakfast was either you or the 'gator) all stereotypes were broken. I met Everly on the last day of Beauty Louisiana. I was tense and tired and he knew what I needed and offered it to me.

We went out into the bayous and back country in his old, beat-up Plymouth station wagon. Roads got narrower and darker, overhung with Spanish moss and lined with dark, sharp palmettos. We got to Boonville about two A.M. It was hot as boiling molasses even at that hour. We rode past his salon, two filling stations, and a grocery store, then turned down a smaller road to his house. He lived in a small, neat house, mostly hidden by live oak trees. As soon as we got into the living room, he lit a kerosene lamp and we took off our sweaty clothes. His large chest was almost covered in thick, black hair that narrowed down to his taut navel and then spread out over his big, thick-stumped dick. He had a lot of Cajun overhang, but as soon as I touched his meat, the head sprang out, glistening like a plum stone.

We had some of the hottest sex I think I've ever had. He had a large, wet tongue, and I knew it wanted to eat every part of me, and it did. I felt the same way about his dick, his ass, his ears and mouth—even his nose. I found myself sucking on his nose and feet, while he was working on other parts of me. He came three times during the night, and what I didn't have of him in my mouth, was soon smeared over much of my body. I'm sure I did the same to him. You could say we spread ourselves very thin during the course of the evening, until the light came up. I fucked him several times, and ended up literally falling asleep with my dick up his ass.

I hate waking up in strange places. It always takes me several hours to feel like I'm myself and haven't turned into somebody else during the night. Of course, if I had been somebody else, Everly and I would have had a lot more sex, especially with him pressing his hard cock down my throat as soon as my eyes opened. Breakfast? I smiled and just sucked him empty.

He made some coffee afterwards, and then we had some eggs and Bloody Marys. "Here's to 'Beauty Louisiana,'" he said, lifting his glass to me. I agreed and said, "'The Self-Expression Factor.' I love it." I laughed.

That evening, he drove me back into the Quarter. There was a letter waiting for me in my mail box, next to the courtyard gate. It was hand delivered, from Jason Benedict. I couldn't wait to tear into it, even though Everly was right there in front of me.

After "Dear Smoky," it said: "I wanted to talk to you in person, but you never seemed to be home. My dad Rollo has agreed to let me go to school up North in Boston. It'll get me out of his hair, but I'll have to leave you. Thanks for the great memories—love...."

"Is that from one of your boyfriends?" Everly asked me. I told him it wasn't. I made some excuse to him that I had a lot of work to do, and said goodbye to him in the courtyard, in front of the door to my carriage house. I watched him disappear down the passageway, and unlock the gate. Then I unlocked the door to my carriage house and sat down at the small table in the living room, that looked out onto my courtyard.

There are certain things you see in your mind over and over again, and I saw Jason lying naked on the flagstones, wet from the hose water and sex. Then I kept repeating to myself—too many times until it didn't make any sense at all to me—"Thanks for the great memories."

THE MOTIVATION

Spence was already half an hour into his talk and I was already bored. I'd heard "Motivation for Success" at least ten times, if not forty—and it wasn't that great the first time, although the audience in that wonderful room in the old Wildlife and Fisheries building on Royale Street was eating it up. The building was a perfect jumble of southern movie baroque, right out of "Gone With the Wind." Even if you couldn't stand the occasion, there was always a fabulous staircase to ascend or descend or just cruise like mad while doing it. This was the Greater New Orleans Tourism and Culture Bureau, that met once a month, and Spence was using it as a way to score new clients for Mondrian, our beauty promo company that was finally pulling itself out of the red.

"Motivation is what makes Success." Blah. Blah. "Motivation is the difference between a thirteen-thousand-dollar-a-year clerk and a three-hundred-thousand-dollar star! How does the Motivated Individual spell success? S is for Sell. U is for Yourself. The first C is for Certainty, and the second C is for Completely. Learn to give of yourself Completely."

I was wondering how I could *completely* get out of there, but it looked like everyone in the room was just eating this up. And why not? Spence hadn't started putting the bite on them yet. That would come later, usually at some point when the pigeon—I mean, client—didn't know what hit him. Mondrian was doing pretty well, at least the company was no longer floating on money from Melissa, Spence's pretty girlfriend with the fat-cat Daddy in Texas. Unfortunately, I was only sitting three rows from the lectern, which meant that Spence or Melissa could see me if I got up. But I'd heard the Motivation speech enough to do it back in my sleep. I could whack off to it, if I had to.

I have found that at times like this—in a large room in a drowsy moment in New Orleans, when you've lost interest completely—the best thing to do is just fall asleep, but not let anyone know it. I have learned to actually fall asleep with my eyes open, but then I started thinking about various men in the room, which ones I would have loved to spend a whole night with, which ones I would have had sex with without going to bed with, which ones in a dark, back room of a bar, let's say, I might just go hog-shit wild with and suck him forty ways to tomorrow, despite the fact that he was fat, ugly, looked like a rodent, but had a nine-inch dick.

Unfortunately, these sort of thoughts are not conducive to any sort of sleep, but they are good for a good hard-on, and I soon forgot all about old Spence yabbering up there. Spence was fat himself, but not ugly—more "seedy" maybe than ugly—and he was giving "Motivation for Success" a good wrap-up just as I was coming back into regular consciousness again.

"Wasn't that just wonderful?" Melissa said to me. She was wearing what they still call down South a "frock," that is, her tits were spilling out of it, and it had several acres of white, eyelet embroidery all over it. Spence was forty-eight and Melissa was twenty years younger, and I was sure that after six years together, with Spence playing Big Daddy and Melissa playing Sugar Girl, eating had completely replaced fucking as the main arena of excitement between them.

I told Melissa that I thought it was the best speech Spence had ever given; then he came up to us and started palavering about all the money in the room—not in the most discrete way (I must say), and I decided right then to split. At least from them. I went to the cash bar and got myself a glass of cold white wine, and then took it to one of the large, open windows, which looked out on to a small square and then Royale Street.

"It's a nice view from here, isn't it?"

I looked up and thought my heart would stop. He was tall and kind of French/German blond—lots and lots of thick, dirty-blond shaggy hair. Deep-set blue eyes, great nose, and then this blond, wonderfully clipped beard to go with it.

I introduced myself and he told me he was Marshall Johnson, and I immediately remembered him from pictures I'd seen in *The Times-Picayune*. He was one of *the* Johnsons, from a plantation family Upriver, who dabbled in the arts, business, and society. Just looking at him, I realized he'd been too scrumptiously gifted by life. There had to be an approachable (alright, we'll call it "vulnerable") link somewhere, not that I am one to bemoan the amusing convergency of magnificent looks, money, and more magnificent looks. He also had a great body—broad T-square shoulders, and long legs. You don't find that *that* often, and I knew it.

"I liked Mr. Butler's speech about Motivation," he went on. "I think being able to sell yourself in this world is very important, don't you?"

Well nothing ventured ... I decided to dive right on in. "I think, Mr. Johnson, you could sell me anything you wanted to."

Suddenly he looked right into my eyes. Now, why are southern men so sexy and flirty? "You can call me Marshall," he said. For a moment, I went blank again. I was trying to think of some way I could get him back to my carriage house in the Quarter. I knew Marshall Johnson was married, but something told me that any man with as many interests as the young Mr. Johnson might be very interesting as well.

Then, to my delight, *he* suggested that we go out for a drink. He was interested in writing, and told me maybe I could give him a few "pointers." I was just about ready to tell him I would point him almost anyplace, when Spence and Melissa suddenly descended on us, like two plump vultures, able to spot money at several hundred yards.

Spence of course started selling him a mile-a-minute. He would be happy to offer Mr. Johnson a "personal motivation course," if he so desired. Marshall started to give me a less than humored look. I was afraid all was lost. Then Melissa suggested we go back to their house on Burgundy Street.

I wasn't sure what to do about this—I mean, who was poaching on whose territory? Marshall had enough money to be a client—without a doubt, Spence could cook up some promotion scheme to snare some of the Johnson money—but I was sure even Spence and Melissa could see that I had the red hots for him, and this was something that was just not going to go away. Marshall looked at me for a moment, then he smiled. Melissa looked at me and winked, and we found a cab outside. It was too hot to walk, and Spence was tired after motivating so many people.

The ride took about six minutes. Their house, which doubled as the Mondrian office, was an impressive number set off slightly from the street. At one time, the place probably had many small rooms, but they were knocked down to produce one very large living room downstairs, that led directly to a beautiful patio, then to an inviting, large, rectangular pool that took up most of the courtyard. The story was that the first owner of the house, after renovation, had had polio, and had actually used the pool to swim in every day.

We plumped down on several large, linen couches in the living room, and Spence took off for the kitchen to whip up a Kool-Aid-sized pitcher of his famous Cajun daiquiris. These were lime, rum, and several good kicks of Tabasco. We started on the daiquiris, then Spence went upstairs and changed into Bermudas, Melissa went into the downstairs bath to do something else, and I went over to Marshall, who seemed rather sheepish and embarrassed now, just to make sure he didn't get lonely. We began with the usual general discussion. His wife was out of town; she'd taken their daughter Holly to Memphis to see her mother. He was going to Monroe Plantation, their "property," the next day.

It was very warm, and the house—which had foot-thick walls and high ceilings, had never been air-conditioned. I suggested that he take off his tie. He did; then I suggested that I'd love to go swimming with him. Right then. He blushed for a moment. Spence came back in and started talking about business. We were always in the market for another "partner." This was his usual pigeon speech. I'd heard it many times before, and was always impressed with the way Spence could bring it off. Totally sincere, but with just enough oil in it—snake oil, maybe—so that you knew he was a professional huckster. Melissa reappeared shortly, in a shorter, more comfortable dress. I knew, like clock-work, that in a couple of minutes, she would get bored with Spence trying to sell the company from under her, and would head upstairs and go to sleep.

I kept hoping that Marshall, though, wouldn't get bored as well. I knew I had to work fast. As I expected, half an hour later, Melissa excused herself and went up to sleep. Now, to get rid of Spence. The best way to do it, I decided, was through Spence's Cajun daiquiris. I had to make sure Marshall didn't get pickled as well. I grabbed the daiquiri pitcher, and kept refilling Spence's glass. His head started to bob around a bit. "You're bein' way too nice to me, Smoky, old man," he kept repeating. I told him he deserved it after such an inspiring speech. Then I jumped quickly into the kitchen— while Spence was slurping through "Motivation means knowing who you are"—and poured about half a fifth of vodka into the daiquiri pitcher, to dilute all the rum. I came out and refilled Spence's glass, completely, one last time. Since cheap vodka is fairly tasteless, in all fairness, I should have been up for an attempted-murder charge. But I knew you couldn't do such things half way in New Orleans.

In about three minutes, Spence went completely "Timber!" I mean *flat*. His eyes were fuzzy. I told him he'd better not even try to climb the stairs into the bedroom. At least by himself. I signaled to Marshall, and together we lifted his legs onto the couch. Seconds later, Spence was out cold, in Bozo-land.

Then Marshall got up. He told me he thought it was time for him to go. I told him flat "No." Now, I suggested, we go for that swim. He objected that he didn't exactly have a swim suit with him.

That was perfectly alright, I told him. It was dark in the courtyard, and the trees surrounding the pool and the walls on all sides made for complete privacy. There was a great, smiling, half-moon up above.

We walked out onto the patio. He paused for a second, and then looked at me. I started to imagine what he would look like naked: from the ground up. Big, sexy feet. Great calves. Knees. Thighs, like you'd want to get lost in. My heart started pounding. It was the only thing I could hear.

"You sure it's okay if we do it this?" he asked.

I didn't answer, but started taking my shirt off, and then unbuckled my belt. I knew I had close to a hard-on and it was going to come ripping out of my Jockey shorts as soon as the head of my dick was exposed to the moist air. I left my shirt and pants on a canvas patio chair, and in just my under-shorts, I began to help him undress. "That's okay," he said, and finished the job himself, very quickly, the way straight men undress in a locker room.

Then, completely stripped, he dove directly into the deep end of the pool, and I followed him. I did have a real hard-on now, and I wanted to start fooling around with him pronto. But I pretended coolness for a second, and just drifted a bit away from him. I turned, and then watched him float-ing, and then swimming, half under the water, white, big and naked, in the almost tropical darkness.

It all seemed so quiet and dream-like that I wanted to pinch myself to make sure I wasn't going to wake up in my bed, soaked in perspiration and cum from a nocturnal jack-off. Sometimes you have to tell yourself that you *have* to believe what's going on—that I really was swimming naked in the pool behind Spence's house; on this gorgeous, breathless hot night in the Quarter; with Marshall Johnson, a married man I'd met only a few hours earlier.

Now he was only an arm's length away from me. I could see his large, uncut cock, wobbling invitingly below the surface of the water. It seemed to be swimming just by itself, with a kind of innocence that was driving me point-blank crazy with horniness for him.

He dove under, so that I could catch the beautiful, white crack of his ass, and then quietly breast-stroked over to me. "It's wonderful here," he said. "I love swimming without clothes on. You really think Spence won't mind?"

"He's asleep. He's just conked out," I said.

"That's nice," he said. His face was just too handsome, with that almost too perfect nose; beautiful, soft lips, and great white teeth. His mop of blonde hair was wet and kept falling into his eyes. I reached over and pushed it away from his face. "Thanks," he said; then I grabbed him around the waist and pulled his beautiful, hard chest closer to me.

"Wait a second," he said. "I'm married, y' know."

I told him I wouldn't hold that against him. The only thing I wanted to hold against him was my cock, which was now pressing right into his balls. My left hand reached under, and I started slowly to stroke his large, smooth nuts, which hung loose in the water.

"Wait a second," he said. "Just wait one second." He started to swim away from me. I felt very embarrassed then, like I'd been reading my signals all wrong. I felt really let down. I got out of the pool and dried myself off with some towels Spence had left on the patio.

I went back into the house. Spence was still asleep in the living room, on the couch. I watched him, then his eyes parted a bit. He narrowed his focus, until he realized he was looking at me. "Are you guys alright out there?" he asked. His eyes opened a bit more. "Are you gettin' it on with him, Smoky? If you need more towels, we have plenty in the bath down here." His eyes closed again.

I smiled, and decided to try one more time. Marshall was still in the pool, at the shallow end away from the house, next to the small, redwood tool-and-pool shed. I dove in and quietly breast-stroked over to him. When I reached him, I didn't know what to say, and I wasn't sure what he was going to do. He just looked at me, then reached out and drew my head closer to his and—without any warning at all—opened his mouth into mine. We held onto each other until the warmth from his body literally ignited me. I thought the water in the pool was going to boil.

"I feel very self-conscious here," he whispered to me. I told him it was alright. His dick, completely hard now, was bigger than I thought. I gently rubbed the head of it in the palm of my hand, and pulled him, at the same time, out of the water.

I remembered that one side of the small tool-and-pool shed had been converted into a sauna. It was unlocked, and I took him inside. It was pitch-black and cold. I flicked on the timed heater, and after a few seconds of clicking noises, the heat came on. There were two redwood benches arranged in tiers for sitting. We were both dripping naked and ravenous the way that only hot, fresh sex can make you—sex without holds, or pasts, or strings attached. I started running my tongue over his smooth chest and hard, firm nipples, while he took my cock into his large, left hand, stroking my ass and back with his right. He sat on the bottom bench, and pulled me closer to him, and then pushed my wild dick into his mouth. I hadn't expected him to suck my cock, or even try to. He had lost all restraints and was senselessly sucking me. I knew I couldn't take that much longer. Just before I blasted, I pulled out and then started eating his full meat. I sat on the sauna bench, and got up and leaned on it with one knee, next to my thigh. I knew then, even while he was pushing his fat rod down my throat, that I wanted his foot in my mouth.

I'd been looking at his feet. They were big, well-made. Really nicely shaped. I grabbed his left foot and just brought it up to my lips and started rimming his toes and the bottom of his foot.

He kept groaning. Satisfied. Excited. The whole range. After I sucked and licked every part of one foot, he let me have the other. Then I began working on his dick again, starting lower with his large, smooth, blond balls. A moment later, we were struggling, rather awkwardly, on the concrete floor, sixty-nining. The head of his cock had swollen to the size of half a fist, but I couldn't stop sucking him for any reason.

Then suddenly he took his cock out of my mouth and inserted his left foot again. I started pumping the big toe into my mouth, then the rest of his toes, in and out, while he jerked himself off. He came in big, white spurts that hit my face. His whole body throbbed. Then I jacked off all over his chest.

We lay for a while on the concrete floor until I realized how hard and gritty it was. I felt numb and delighted at the same time. We went back into the pool and I kissed him some more. "Do you think Spence is up?" he asked me. He told me, very bashfully, that he just wanted to walk out without embarrassing anyone.

We put our clothes back on and without waking Spence downstairs or Melissa upstairs, got out of the house. Burgundy Street was still alive with men cruising either on foot or in cars. Marshall pretended that he didn't notice what was going on, although a great number of eyes were on him. We walked back towards my carriage house, three blocks away. For one of the few moments during my time in New Orleans, I felt stunned into silence. I didn't want to say the wrong thing. I didn't want to talk about his wife or the weather, or say, "I hope I'll see you again," when I knew there was little chance of it. I didn't want this tiny, beautiful slice of time I had with Marshall Johnson to evaporate into some stupid talk.

"I'm glad I listened to Spence's Motivation speech," he said to me in front of the gate to my courtyard. "I never would have had the courage to do what I just did, if I hadn't."

He suddenly broke into a large, nice smile. I winked at him and then quickly kissed him. I wanted so much to hold his lips close to mine, but I couldn't. He quickly broke away from me, then grabbed a cab at the corner of St. Phillip and Dauphine Street, back to his house uptown.

THE MAN WITH THE CALIFORNIA FACE

3

It was February in New York and I was sitting on the subway coming back from a job uptown that I was already getting tired of. The subway car wasn't too crowded for rush hour—that is, there was still some breathing space left in it. I was tired of the cold weather and the even colder people in their heavy, dirty winter clothes, the down parkas shiny with sweat stains and the cheap fur coats bought at bargain prices last winter. There was a lady sitting next to me who looked as if her rabbit coat had died very shortly after the rabbits did. Great chunks of rabbit fur had come out of it, and the coat looked so pathetic that I thought it needed a funeral, along with the poor rabbits who'd given themselves up for it. Alright. I guess you've figured this out: I—and most of New York—was ready for the end of winter. We were screaming for it. I was ready for all the frozen dog shit on the street to melt in the spring thaw, and for night to stop blasting in at four thirty in the afternoon.

I can't remember exactly what I was thinking—perhaps it was that recurrent feeling that New York was getting to be more of a punishment than a city, or that I was just getting bad at taking it, when I noticed him standing directly across from me. At first, it was just the back of his head, very thick, curly, salt-and-pepper gray, that attracted me. But I noticed that it was more silver than salt, and even the pepper part had a kind of Scandinavian silkiness to it that wasn't quite blond, but was hardly brown either. It was almost a pewter color. He was tall, but well built. I could tell that even under the *good* fur coat he was wearing. It was a large, dark number—maybe sable for all I knew. But he looked great in it. Tall men, especially with this man's coloring, wear fur coats well. He was wearing heavy, black leather boots, the kind more for riding than for snow. They were well shined, like he'd taken some pains to keep the winter salt off them, which, if you're not careful, will destroy riding boots very quickly in our hunting forests of Manhattan. The thought of him on a horse made me want to hunt as well, and I certainly don't mean for the type of rabbits the lady next to me was wearing.

I wondered what the front of him looked like. That seemed like a fairly normal thought when you're facing such an attractive looking back picture on a New York subway. I found myself just looking at him, and smiling to myself. I have found that simply looking at people—especially very attractive men—has a calming effect on me. It tends to take anxiety away, and I tend to get anxious in subway crowds. This is not the best trait to have in the city, but there were far worse ones and I have managed to stay pretty much alive even with this one.

A moment later, after I had memorized every line of the back of his coat, and the way his sharp gabardine pants strained over his calves, the person sitting down next to him got up. He turned around casually, looked directly in front, and saw me. I was sitting at the end of one of those seats that run along the entire sides of some cars. They're designed for maximum standing room, and minimum comfort. Our eyes locked for an embarrassing moment. I tried to turn away from him, but I couldn't. The magnetism was already there. I couldn't deny it. As much as I *didn't* want him to know how much I was thinking about him, turning away from his face—which seemed so open and trusting and warm—was impossible for me to do. It was too cold that winter, and I wanted all the warmth I could get.

His face was attractive. Warm, large mouth. Thin, chiseled nose. Glowing eyes. His eyes, even more than the handsomeness of his face, held me. They didn't flinch or turn away from me, like most New York eyes do. Neither did they try to stare me down. Instead, his eyes led me on, held me, told me something.

144

I wasn't sure what to do. I was having such a rush of interest in him. For a moment, the subway disappeared. It was as if on some fantasy level, I was already with him, undressing him, exploring all the places on his warm body. My lips ran down his heavy, horse-muscular neck. They produced a ripple of pleasure every place they touched him. He sighed; smiled. I wondered what his nipples felt like in my mouth, what his cock looked like.

Tasted like. The fantasy became warm and dark; I knew that he was pulling me into it, just from the way he looked at me. I wondered if he could see it on my face, that I was already exploring his body, that any moment I'd have his cock in my mouth.

The train hit Times Square. I was exploded back into reality. The car bristled with people. Two teenaged Latino boys sprinted into the empty seat by him. If you wanted to sit, you had to be fast. He was carrying two shopping bags in his left hand. He moved forward, closer to me. We still looked at each other. My skin started to burn. My heart beat faster. He moved about two inches closer. Another moment and my ears would vibrate. They did this when I got really turned on, from the rush of blood into them. More people squashed in, fortunately pushing him towards me. Now he stood directly in front. I looked up at him and knew my face was red. Fantasies weren't supposed to get this real.

He smiled slightly. His legs pressed into my knees. I thought I was going to pee in my pants from the tension. I couldn't believe the whole subway car wasn't staring at me, and that every man, woman, and kid over the age of six didn't know how much I wanted him. The noise as we pulled out of the station was deafening. But some of it—I realized—was my heart pumping.

I took a deep breath. "Do you want to sit down?" I asked him. Maybe he hadn't heard me. The train screeched. The lady in the moth-eaten rabbits started nervously shifting her legs. Did this mean she was on to what was going on? I've always felt that New Yorkers have a special sense—like street X-ray vision. They can see right through you. So could Miss Rabbit tell how much I wanted to flip this guy into the sack? Suddenly she clutched her purse, got up, and took her dead rabbits with her. Her place next to me was now empty. I was relieved.

"Do you want to sit down?" I said again. But before he could answer, a very nervous Asian man planted himself in the empty seat. He flicked open a Chinese newspaper; I felt better. There was more than a decent chance that he couldn't tell anything I was feeling or saying.

The man in the sable coat leaned over towards me. His cheek stood about half an inch from mine. I could feel his breath. It felt cool; fragrant. "No thank you," he said in a soft, low voice. "I'm getting off in two stops."

"So am I," I said.

He continued to look at me. "Good," he whispered.

I realized that I was already getting hard. I felt my cock swell up inside my briefs. It warmed my left thigh as it pressed against it. I stared ahead and looked, for a moment, directly into his crotch covered by his fur coat. He raised his right knee slightly. His body language was direct. The heat in the car went up considerably. My legs started to tremble. From where I sat, there were all sorts of body parts around me: legs, fannies, elbows almost in

145

my face. Suddenly, they became simply that: just body parts. I decided *no* one was looking. The body parts weren't connected to brains. And if they were, the brains didn't have to pay any attention to me. I'd gone from shy to hard. This was New York, where people are always busy making money, or deciding how to spend it. What *I* did should be of little interest to them. I felt better after my attitude change.

We came to Penn Station. A horde of commuters got off. The next stop was Fourteenth Street. It was not really my stop; but why not? The train reared off again as I squirmed in my seat a bit, and then suddenly put my hand under his fur coat.

I could tell he was hard, too. I felt him for a second. The doors snapped open once more: instantly I popped up; then we were both out of the train. I didn't say anything else, but followed him.

We got out on Fifteenth Street. A zing of snapping cold air woke me fully from this day dream of hot sex fantasies I'd been walking through. It was like a light, affectionate slap. He was taller than me, by about three inches. I'm five-foot-ten. He seemed bigger now, or maybe I just felt smaller. I wasn't sure what to do next. We didn't say anything for a few minutes.

Then he stopped and looked at me. Now was the real shit-or-get-off-the-pot moment, and I knew it. I could invite him for a drink, make up some-thing. I had certainly picked up guys before. I stood there for a second, and tried to come up with a line. I wanted to seem like I was in some control of myself. I didn't want to come off like a perfect klutz. "Do you want to come home with me?" he asked.

I smiled. A mild, nice kind of shock ran through me. It was the kind of feeling you might have if you cruised a cop who winked back at you. It's like you didn't expect it to happen, but it's nice. There was supposed to be all sorts of crap leading up to this. Games, hints, shit like that. Now what to do? I didn't want to think about it. There were a lot of things to think about, stuff I was supposed to be doing at the moment. I knew that. "Sure," I said. "I'd really like to."

"I'm just staying around the corner," he told me.

I told him that was nice. We walked down two more blocks. A stiff wind started howling between buildings. The blocks were dark and cold. He looked at me and smiled, which made the short walk warmer. I asked him where he was from. He told me he was only visiting from California, San Diego, to be exact. "The person I'm staying with is out of town at the moment," he explained. Now I could feel my temperature rise when he told me this. Despite the drop in temperature outside, inside I was getting a *lot* hotter.

The place he took me to was very luxurious; at least by my standards. I was used to East Village hole-in-the-walls, with cockroaches for pets and bathtubs stuck in the kitchen. He was staying in a floor-through on East Sixteenth Street, just east of Union Square. It was in a beautiful old town house, with lots of elaborate, turn-of-the-century details, like cute Cupids carved in marble over the doorway. He told me his name was Curt when he unlocked the door and I entered a foyer with an inlaid, hardwood floor.

"Curt," I said and let his name roll around in my mouth. I smiled and asked him if I should take off my coat, which was a simple, leather bomber jacket. "At least that," he said and I smiled a bit more "Do you want something to drink?" he asked, and I said sure. "All we have is Scotch," he said. "Scotch or Mexican beer."

I told him beer was fine, and he went down a long hallway into the kitchen to get it. I looked around the living room. Nicely done. In the middle was a heavy, dark leather couch—the kind you could see yourself lying on, wrapped naked in a fur throw. Naked was always better, I thought. I noticed several deep wing chairs, tall oak bookcases, thick oriental rugs. The masterpiece of the room though was a huge fireplace. The sort that only older buildings had, when people actually used fireplaces for heat. You could roast an ox in it.

"Your friend has good taste," I said as he came back in with two tall beer glasses filled with cold, foaming beer. He'd stuck small slices of lime in the glasses, a very nice touch I thought.

"Not exactly my *friend*," he said. "We used to be married." He offered the beer to me. "Some of this stuff used to be mine. It was thrown into our ..." He paused for a second, then said with a sigh, "our divorce settlement. Part of the settlement was that I get to use this place a few times a year. Usually my *ex* heads out when I do."

It didn't sound like the friendliest divorce to me, but who was I to judge? I'd never been married, *or* divorced. I sat down on the couch and looked at him again—now that he didn't have his fur coat on. He must have noticed that my eyes stayed on him.

"Is everything alright?" he asked.

"No."

"What's wrong?"

"I want to see you with your clothes off," I said. "Think you can arranged that?"

His head jerked suddenly, like he wasn't sure he'd heard what I said, then he gave me a very sheepish smile. I got up from the couch and began to unbutton the simple, white silk shirt he was wearing. His chest was very broad and fairly hairless. When I opened the third button, my hand reached in and started to play with his nipples, squeezing them gently.

"That's nice," he said. "I like being undressed."

I told him I did, too. I wasn't sure what sort of bedroom arrangement

Curt had with the ex-Mrs. Curt. Maybe their divorce settlement had included that he wasn't supposed to discover *her* dildos under the bed.

"Do you use your ex's bedroom, too?" I asked.

"Sometimes. But why don't I build a fire here? It's nice in front of the fire."

He'd already built quite a fire inside of me, but the idea of making love in front of that really beautiful fireplace on a really wretched cold night when before I'd been expecting to go home and eat a TV dinner alone—well, it was a great idea. I drank some more beer and he put several logs that were resting by the fireplace onto the andirons, then put some kindling wood under the logs.

"This kindling's very good," he explained. "It gets things very hot."

I merely nodded yes. What could I say after a line like that? I stripped off my sweater and the cotton flannel shirt under it. He seemed pleased with the dark hair on my chest. Then I took off my shoes, socks, jeans, and underwear. I liked the idea of being totally naked right there in front of him.

He began to finish unbuttoning his shirt. I told him to wait a second. The fire started to crackle and spit loudly. It was the only light in the room. "Why don't you lie down there on the rug?" I said. I drew the fire screen closed. I felt there were going to be enough sparks flying between the two of us. He stretched out on the rug, with his shirt open. I began licking his neck, and—exactly as I imagined—a line of excited gooseflesh followed my tongue. I could feel the hard, cord-like muscles of his neck vibrate just a bit where my lips touched them.

My mouth went further, following the line of his neck and upper chest to his hard nipples. I bit each one just enough to cause them to ridge up. I pulled his shirt out of his pants, and raised it, completely unbuttoned over his head. I began to lick his underarms, they were full of pale hair that looked blonde, even gold in the firelight.

"Maybe I should take my pants off now," he said. "I wouldn't want to come all over them.

Nice thought—that he was that hot. I unzipped his fly, while he fondled, almost tickling it, the large head of my cock. I'm uncut, but have almost no foreskin, and the head was starting to shine with excitement. I knelt over him, so that my dick was close to his handsome face, and he quickly licked the head and then put some of it into his warm, soft mouth. I reached back and pulled his dick and balls out of his pants. His cock was very long and thin, but with a large, curious head. It seemed to have a fat life of its own. It reminded me of the swollen, sexy buds of peonies. The buds are always very thick on a thin stem.

"You're very hot," I said to him.

He smiled as my cock came out of his mouth. He got up and his pants dropped as far as they could. His boots kept them from going any further than his calves.

"I've got to take these off," he said. I felt disappointed. I didn't want his boots off. They were too nice looking. But I helped him unbuckle the three, outer side buckles on each boot, so that they slid easily off his feet. He got his pants off, then a pair of white, Jockey briefs. His ass looked pale, silvery in the fire light. I grabbed both of his firm butt cheeks with my hands and held him close to me. I was still on my knees. I closed my eyes and kissed the round, firm mounds of his sweet butt. I faced him then. His hands grabbed the thick, curly hair of my head.

My heart started beating really fast. I knew what I wanted to do. I wanted to make love with him with those hot, sexy boots on. I was naked and I wanted him that way—but with his boots on. He'd kept his socks on. My lips started to suck the silver gray hairs on his large, crinkly balls. One of his testicles found its way into my mouth, while my hand ran over the thin length of his shaft. I bit very softly into his ball.

He let out a slow, deep groan of pleasure. I dropped his ball from my mouth. "Like that?" I asked.

"Sure."

"I want you to put your boots back on," I said.

He smiled. "Whatever you say," he said. "If you keep my balls in your mouth, you can do anything you like."

"I want you to put your boots back on," I said and slapped his ass with a firm hand. I brought his boots back over to him and put them on him, buckling them after they were on his feet.

"God, you look nice," I said. "Why don't you walk around a bit?"

He walked over to the fireplace and drew the fire screen open. He took the poker and started to play with the fire, while his dick flopped around very hard in the air. I thought I was in hog-heaven ecstasy just looking at him.

When he finished with the fire, he drew the screen back and I told him that I wanted to grease his boots up.

"What?" he asked, smiling.

"Grease up your boots. Do you have any leather lubricant?" I always used a natural, bear-fat lubricant on mine. It was made in Canada, and the smell, slightly musky and tangy at the same time, drove me crazy. If I had had any with me, I think I would have eaten it right off his boots.

"You people in New York are nuts," he said and started rolling with laughter. He went into the kitchen and came back with a tin of vegetable shortening. "I just use this," he said. "It's got all sorts of uses, know what I mean?"

Crisco was definitely not as sexy as bear grease, but probably better for

149

my digestive gut in the long run—unless I was interested in sprouting a bear rug all over my back, which I wasn't partial to. I opened the can and got down on my knees again, and began to rub the grease into his boot with my fingers and the heels of the palms of my hands. The leather softened under my hands and my cock dragged along the calves and tops of his boots, picking up some of the Crisco along the way.

Suddenly he grabbed my balls and stuck my dick again into his mouth. I knew there was nothing I could do then. The guy just wanted my cock. The fire prickled my ass with it's jumping heat, while we sixty-nined on the silky, Persian rug in front of the fireplace. After a few minutes of sucking his meat, I started licking his boots and jerking him off with my greased hands. The smell of the oiled leather was as exciting as having his cock in my mouth. I couldn't control myself any longer and grabbing my wet dick out of his mouth, I used my other hand to jerk myself off all over his boots. My cum glistened on both of the slick, greased boots until I rubbed it into the grease.

Then I sucked him some more, until he decided it was time to shoot. He pulled his meat out of my mouth, and jerked off into my chest hairs. He smiled for a second, then started licking his jism off my nipples. I put his dick back into my mouth, getting just one more taste of him before we settled down in front of the fire.

The fire seemed brighter and hotter now. I was panting and out of breath. He got up and got us some more beer. When he came back, he'd taken his hunky boots off.

"You're very good looking," I said to him, as I watched the fire light play over his naked, tall body, his broad chest, long legs, and beautiful, dangling cock.

"Thank you."

"Your wife must have been a lucky woman," I said.

He smiled. "What wife? Women are not the only things you marry nowadays. I was with him for ten years. It just didn't work out. I started to feel he was only interested in money—money and who he knew. That was it. So I went out to California. I only wear that heavy fur coat when I come here in the winter."

The two of us stretched out again by the fire. There was something I really liked about this guy. I cupped his head in my hands and felt the silvery softness of his hair. He smiled at me. I opened my mouth and kissed him, pulling his tongue into mine. Then I said, "I'm glad you decided to stay the way you are. I mean, even if you did have to leave New York to do it."

"Thanks," he said. He closed his eyes and his lips turned up in a soft smile while he relaxed in the warmth of the fire and the touch of my hands on his chest. I started to kiss his chest again. His eyes opened, as if he'd been startled pleasantly out of a dream.

I stopped what I was doing and looked at him. He seemed so open and sweet that I wanted to eat every part of him. "You are the man with the California face," I said. I began to kiss him again, while he only smiled.

A note about the brands: the branding iron symbols used at the opening of each story are traditional branding marks from the years of the old West and the open range. They include such brands as the the Rocking K, the Rocking H, the Fork E, the Cosmic Turtle, the Golden Shower, and the ever-popular Lazy W. We hope that you enjoyed them, and that every fan of Smoky George will find a brand of his own that he—or she—can claim.

Perry Brass

Although Perry Brass was born in Savannah, Georgia in 1947, he has lived much of his adult life in the North East. He has been at the forefront of gay writing for twenty years. He was an editor of *Come Out!*, the first gay liberation newspaper in the world, published by New York's Gay Liberation Front. His poetry and essays, some of the most influential in the early years of the gay movement, were published in San Francisco's *Gay Sunshine*, in the famous, underground *Gay Flames Packet*, and in alternative papers nationally. He was included in *The Male Muse*, the first public anthology of gay poetry; and collections like Gay Sunshine Press' *Angels of the Lyre;* the controversial *Penguin Book of Homosexual Verse; The New Gay Liberation Book* (Ramparts Press); *Gay Liberation* (the anthology from Rolling Stone Press, that included work by John Lennon); and *Out of the Closets*, recently re-released by New York University Press.

His short stories, poems, and essays have appeared in *Christopher Street, The New York Native, Amethyst, Mouth of the Dragon, Invert, Alfred Hitchcock Magazine*, and many smaller literary magazines. His plays and performance pieces have been performed in New Orleans, New York, Chicago, and Los Angeles. In 1985, his play "Night Chills," one of the first plays to deal with the AIDS crisis, won the Jane Chambers International Gay Playwriting Contest. His two-man work, "All Men," taken from twenty years of his writing, ran Off-Broadway at Wings Theatre Company in New York. His collaborations with composer Chris DeBlasio have included "Five Prayers," commissioned by the New Orleans Gay Men's Chorus, and "All The Way Through Evening," an elegiac song cycle based on five poems that has been performed by major singers in many American cities and Europe.

His first book of poems, *Sex-charge*, was published in Jan., 1991, by Belhue Press. Christopher Hewitt writing in **The New York Native** said, "All in all, these poems do more than merely celebrate gay male sexuality; they portray the love and literary/ historical tradition of male bonding as *noble, infinitely deep and infinitely enduring.*"

Mirage, his gay science fiction thriller, became an underground best-seller in the U.S. and England. *Mirage* is the story of Enkidu and Greeland, two men from the distant, tribal planet Ki, who are forced to Earth where they take over the bodies and identities of two male lovers. *Mirage* was nominated for a Lambda Literary Award for Gay Men's Science Fiction.

Perry Brass is a member of the Dramatists Guild, The Small Press Association, and currently lives in Connecticut.

MIRAGE

ELECTRIFYING SCIENCE FICTION BY PERRY BRASS

On the tribal planet *Ki*, two men—in the spirit of an ancient pact—have been promised to each other for a lifetime. But a savage attack and murder break this promise and force them to seek another world where imbalance and lies form Reality. This is the planet known as Earth, a world they will use and escape.

Mirage tells the story of Greeland, an ambitious hunter from the rich forests of Ki, and his overwhelming love for his younger friend, Enkidu. Greeland's love must survive this charge of murder, their escape to Earth—through the properties of a powerful third testicle, called **The Egg of the Eye**—and their new lives in cities, taking over the bodies and identities of two earth-bound lovers, Alan and Wright.

Mirage was nominated for a 1992 Lambda Literary Award for Best Gay Men's Science Fiction/Fantasy.

"*Mirage* goes further than its predecessors ... it combines science fiction, gay reality, ... and maleroticism in one neat package. ... In Ki, Brass has (re)fashioned a gaymale fantasy as old as the *Epic of Gilgamesh* and as recent as our dreams. Those who like sex with their science fiction should note that *Mirage* has some of the hottest scenes on two planets." Jesse Monteagudo in **The Weekly News**, Miami, Florida.

"What we've got here is four characters in two bodies ... a startling historical perspective on sexual politics ... intelligent and intriguing." Bob Satuloff in the **New York Native.**

Mirage. 224 pages. $10.95
ISBN 0-9627123-1-0

SEX-CHARGE

ACCLAIMED POETRY FROM PERRY BRASS

Joan Rivers meets Liz Taylor. Jesse Helms meets Robert Mapplethorpe. From drag queens to suburban gay daddies, everybody meets in *Sex-charge*, Perry Brass' outrageous book of gay poetry, accompanied with striking male photos by Manhattan photographer Joe Ziolkowski. Nominated 1992 Lambda Literary Award for <u>Best Gay Men's Poetry</u>.

"This is a rich, diverse collection of poems, perceptive, sometimes funny, sometimes resonant, and accessible to any intelligent reader, even the one who doesn't usually go for poetry. Though its themes are varied, it's also a strongly gay collection, and—much needed in these times—strongly erotic." Ian Young in **Mandate**.

" ...poetry at it's highest voltage ... the poet ransacks every personal and universal element that makes everybody's primal urge and surging culmination dance down the page and into our heads, hearts, and gonads ... Brass' particular talent is his ability to ... create a distinctive verse that communicates to everyone." Marv. Shaw in **Bay Area Reporter**.

Sex-charge. 76 pages. $6.95. With sensitive male photos by Joe Ziolkowski.
ISBN 0-9627123-0-2

At your bookstore, or from:

Belhue Press
P.O. Box 1081
Ridgefield, CT 06877-0842

Please add 2.00 shipping each first book, and $1.00 for each book thereafter. CT residents please add 8% sales tax. Foreign orders in U.S. currency only.